HITCH AMERICA

Anno Domini 1978

Richard Wynter

Published by New Generation Publishing in 2021

First Edition

Paperback ISBN: 978-1-80031-386-6
Ebook ISBN: 978-1-80031-385-9

www.newgeneration-publishing.com

New Generation Publishing

FOREWORD

Sitting in my garden on a hot August afternoon while enjoying a socially-distanced catch up with my cousin Richard, I could not have imagined any more surprises than I'd already experienced during 2020.

Until, that is, Richard announced he was writing a book.

'I was wondering if you would read it for me,' he said. 'I know you'll give me an honest appraisal, good or bad, and any suggestions would be much appreciated!

'I've been writing it on and off for ten years and lockdown's given me the opportunity to finally get it finished!' he added, while I absorbed this startling bit of news.

In May 1978, as a green behind the ears, fresh out of college, driven by the desire to escape the shackles of a restrictive home life and the suffocation of the humdrum life of back-street Hastings, where future prospects seemed extremely limited, Richard and his good chum Steve Elder flew to New York. Armed with a map, tent and a budget of just $3 a day, without a plan or a care in the world, but with a desire to broaden themselves culturally, socially and sexually, they embarked on a seven-month odyssey hitchhiking across the United States, Canada and Mexico.

I was fifteen at the time he took off and my only memory of him was his abundance of wild curly hair and incessant chat about cricket. I had no idea what he had got up to during those months as he had never spoken about it, so I was intrigued to read the first draft he left with me that day.

It doesn't take too many pages to realise that Richard can write and has a sense of humour even funnier than I had appreciated. From the moment Richard and Stevie board the Freddie Laker Sky Train at Gatwick, with just £500 of hard currency in the form of traveller's cheques, the reader is taken on a journey of discovery.

His amusing, anecdotal and descriptive way of writing through the eyes of an unworldly twenty-one-year-old Englishman that until landing in America had never eaten pizza, regarding it as foreign muck, is compelling, and you actually feel you are on the road with him and his mate, living the moments as they happened.

From landing in New York, the lads proceed to thumb their way across North America via Vancouver Island, the south-west states to Mexico back to Texas. They visit well-known tourist spots as well and numerous obscure places and Richard's descriptions of the landscapes, towns and cities are vivid and insightful with a sufficient amount of interesting facts to make the reader feel they have learnt something. The reader also gains a real insight into life in America forty-odd years ago, elements of which appear no different from today and the various people they encounter along the way provide an interesting and colourful backdrop to the journey. From ordinary citizens and distant relations they had never met to campers, hippies, druggies, hoodlums, gun-toting drivers, hookers and bears and bulls. There are many moments in the book which make you draw breath and also make you laugh out loud, which is a real winner for me.

No matter what your age, this travelogue offers something for everyone and for anyone thinking about undertaking a similar adventure in the future it provides plenty of inspiration and leaves you believing anything is possible. I can also see how this was a journey of self-discovery for Richard and I believe it helped shape him into the man he is today, best known for his lifelong passion and support of Sussex County Cricket Club.

I am extremely proud to have been asked to collaborate on this book and even prouder to be able to write this foreword on my cousin's behalf. I really hope you enjoy reading it as much as I have.

Francesca Green.
25th October 2020

CHAPTERS

1. Montague Burton And The Absolute Duffers

I couldn't quite believe it; I had to have misheard him.

'You're going where?'

'America and Canada! Me and the Reverend...'

'You, Stevie? And Marcus Ball hitchhiking?'

Stevie nodded. 'Yep! New York to Boston, Buffalo, Ohio, Chicago, Denver, Seattle, San Francisco and LA, Texas, Florida, Georgia, Virginia, DC and all points in between.'

Steve Elder and the 'Reverend' Marcus Ball were hitchhiking around North America after the summer term. I didn't see that one coming.

Although I was perplexed by this seismic change of routine, my immediate feeling was one of tremendous envy. Ever since I was a small lad I'd had a hankering to visit the United States of America. I guess growing up in the sixties I was exposed to a diet of American movies and the stars and stripes. Huge cities full of skyscrapers, ten-lane freeways and a country of vast landscapes. Hollywood always seemed to depict the States in a glamorous light; even the gangsters had an aura and magnetism not replicated by the Pinewood studios of Borehamwood. Of course the old Westerns were classical: deserts, mountains, deep river gorges, two-bit towns and the saloon bars. Everyone carried a gun and spoke with a strange drawl and wore silly hats. I found it perplexing that these old Westerns, traditionally set in the latter half of the nineteenth century, always featured clean-cut cowboys with short back and sides!

A more unlikely pair than Steve, or Stevie as he was often known, and Marcus hitchhiking together I really could not imagine. To the best of my knowledge Stevie had never been out of Bexhill for more than a day. He had certainly never been north of Watford, let alone North America and it seemed wholly out of character to hitchhike anywhere. Steve gave a good impression of being low on confidence and self-belief. Well, impressions can be deceptive. As for Marcus Ball, it seemed even more bizarre. Equally unadventurous, the son of an eccentric snob, Marcus was a junior eccentric snob, although a decent lovable bloke, somewhat naïve, but intensely ostentatious, verging on the ridiculous. The previous Christmas he told me he was going on a 'turkey shoot' to bag his Christmas lunch. It turned out he bagged his turkey in the freezer cabinet of the local 'Iceland' freezer centre. That was classic Marcus.

I think all our mates were curiously amused at the thought of Stevie and Marcus setting off to conquer the United States of America. But they were determined to go and prove to themselves that anything was possible. For myself I didn't pay any outward attention to it but, inside, I was full of admiration for them and wondered why I hadn't thought about such an epic adventure. The answer was of course that the whole idea was so surreal, it just would not have occurred to me any more than becoming an international test cricketer, an Oxbridge professor or a captain of industry. Cooped up in little old Hastings on the south coast of Sussex you just did not do that sort of thing. Life for us was generally something that happened elsewhere, to other people from the metropolises with a wider vision and greater perspective. So I fell in with the majority view that it would be very interesting to hear how they progressed and let my attentions drift towards another lazy three months' summer holiday by the English Channel.

Let me introduce myself. I am Richard Wynter, Rich or Richie (a parody on Richie Benaud who was a bit of a cult hero), but more often than not just plain old Richard. A late baby boomer originally from Carshalton Beeches, my family had moved to Hastings when I was six. I loved the seaside, the salt air and the shrill of the seagulls and took pride in the history of Hastings, the old ruined castle, 1066 and all that. It is curious really that the Hastings devotees took such a paradoxical pride in the Norman Conquest, as it was the last time the British Isles were successfully invaded; it just had to be at Hastings!

The Battle of Hastings put the town firmly on the map and Hastings Tourist Board tried to make the most of it in its holiday advertising campaigns. Conversely, the French were much despised and mistrusted in Hastings. There was a very amusing local headline back in the sixties when a couple of French teenagers were caught shoplifting at Plummers, the town's department store. *The Hastings & St Leonards Observer* banner headline read 'The French Still At It Nine Hundred Years On'. I remember this tickled my mother no end. The nine-hundredth anniversary of the famous battle in 1966 was a big event for the town. The Queen visited the town and was paraded along the seafront in a gleaming Rolls Royce; a replica of the Bayeux Tapestry was commissioned and exhibited on Hastings Pier; a full set of British postage stamps, depicting scenes from the Bayeux Tapestry was issued to commemorate the occasion and a re-enactment of the battle was staged at Battle Abbey on the site of the original carnage on 14th October. Far more people came than was expected and the stallholders couldn't keep up with demand for tea and cakes, and this time round the Saxons scored a home victory, much to general approval. The Anglo-Saxons were back in charge!

My father had a far more personal reason for disliking the French and Charles de Gaulle in particular. Having buggered off to Dublin at the first sign of trouble in 1940, de Gaulle returned to Paris to a hero's welcome in 1945 after British and American repatriation without a word of thanks to the allies. Dad never forgave him for that, as he was in France risking his life, while de Gaulle was on the Guinness. I had a lot of empathy with my father's point of view.

However, none of this decreased the general air of decay and defeatism that hung over the Hastings and St Leonards area right through the 1960s and 70s. As a teenager, the reality of living in the town was quite depressing. It was quiet, humdrum, backward, tedious and completely lacking in opportunity. There were still many old Second World War bombsites around the town left barren thirty years on. My father especially recognised the failings of the town in the modern era, as he had come here as a small boy in the early thirties with his parents on summer holidays. Back then he told me Hastings had been a forward thinking, progressive and dynamic town. The town had a reputation for breaking new boundaries: for example a funicular was installed on both the East and West Hill from Hastings seafront in 1902 and powered by water. A sea-defence was installed in the early thirties, called 'Bottle Alley' which was unheard of back then, to stop the town from flooding during winter storm surges. Also Hastings had the first underground car park anywhere in the world built at the same time. The crowning glory during that inter-war period was the development of the imposing Marina Court building on the seafront at St Leonards-on-Sea. A classic Art Deco construction, it was loosely based on the *Queen Mary* luxury cruise liner built with rounded stern and tiered balconies, just like the real thing. During the Sixties the stern part housed a night club called the 'Cobweb', where famously Jimi Hendrix once performed. It still looks original even now in the seventies. But the point was that in those thirty years since the end of the Second World War Hastings had deteriorated, nothing had progressed and the old bombsites typified the stagnation.

My local school in St Leonards-on-Sea was a mirror image of the town, a borstal in all but name and I hated it. Full of thugs and yobbos where education was a misnomer; fights, bullying, muggings, truant and a damn good daily kicking was the everyday norm. However, the ultimate act of intimidation and humiliation was to be thrown down the bank. The 'bank' was a muddy ten to twelve-foot slope covered in nettles and brambles at the back of the large 'playground'. At the bottom of the bank was an even muddier ditch bordered by gorse bushes. If there were five hundred boys at the school, in the course of a year at least four hundred of them would experience the bank treatment. I reckoned in my four years I had the indignity of being chucked down the bank six or seven times. A new headmaster was appointed in 1970. His name was Cameron Bray known throughout the entire school as 'Donkey'. He was a classic 'do-gooder' and he easily identified the main school bullies and made them prefects 'to give them responsibility'. The bullies understood this to mean 'to give them authority', so to be chucked down the bank now seemed to have official backing. It was horrible. Seven or eight louts would grab your wrists and ankles and swing you over the precipice. 'One, two, three' they roared and let go. It ruined my clothes. I was stung, scratched and bruised but not half as much as my ego. The 'bank' initiations always seemed to draw a crowd a bit like bear baiting or a good old-fashioned gallows hanging. Teacher intervention just didn't happen: I suspect one or two feared they would be chucked down the bank too.

Schooling at the Grove Secondary Modern on Wishing Tree Road was for others and not to be encouraged by the hordes of gangs who felt it was their God-given right to prevent the development of knowledge, intellectual improvement, tuition and broadened horizons. I had always thought of myself as a pretty good judge of character, which is why I vehemently hated most of my fellow school chums. The Grove had a lot to answer for as the teachers were not in control. It wasn't really their fault they weren't up to it. The juvenile thugs just had no interest in their own futures. Teacher torment was rife, from just good old backchat, harassment and disobedience to locking dear old 'Arnie' the RK teacher in his stock cupboard all night, which happened on more than one occasion. Teachers came and went as most, understandably, didn't like the boys under their tutelage and one or two liked them a bit too much. Having left school at the first opportunity at the tender age of fifteen, with a mind uncluttered with knowledge and a total qualification count of exactly zero, I was just another statistic in the failure column of the British educational system and of course totally unprepared for the real world.

Montague Burton Limited, Gentlemen's Tailors and Outfitters, came to my rescue. They had advertised in the *Hastings & St Leonards Observer* for a junior sales assistant; suitable for someone with drive, enthusiasm, personality, numeracy and literacy. Well this wasn't me as I had not acquired any of these basic requirements, but I was a junior member of Sussex County Cricket Club and that seemed to be qualification enough for the manager, Mr Upton. I was employed at £7.75 per week, before tax and National Insurance deductions. I was asked to sweep the stairs each day, polish the brass fittings, make tea on the hour, keep the stock tidy and when demand was high serve the customers. Most of the time work was tedious and repetitive. However, before September was out, I had been elevated to Mr Upton's Sunday first XI, where he just happened to be both chairman and captain and was given a bat and a bowl. I was reasonably good at cricket and had captained the Grove School first XI while still in my fourth and final year.

Saturdays were enlivened by the presence of the part-time cashier, Emma. A woman twice my age, with a deep husky voice; she oozed sex appeal and had a body to kill for and a husband who would have killed anybody who got anywhere near. I was fascinated by her wonderful bosom, which was quite magnetic and hypnotic to the point she had to tell me to look her in the eye when talking to her, not the chest! Despite my fixation, Emma seemed to take a maternal interest in me. She encouraged me to stand up for myself, question, and challenge and argue my corner. I knew this to be good advice and tried my best to take it on board. Although I did grow in confidence, after two years of measuring inside legs and selling exactly the same suit to half the population of Hastings and St Leonards-on-Sea, I was getting restless and needed a more stimulating challenge.

My parents were very concerned at my lack of formal qualifications and career prospects. They were insistent I go to college to 'catch up' and obtain some basic 'O' and 'A' levels. The thought of returning to any educational establishment filled me with dread.

However, when my best mate at the time, Adrian, a fellow refugee of the Grove School, sided with Mum and Dad, I started to take the idea more seriously. If a fellow seventeen-year-old and good friend agreed it was the right thing to do, then I guess it was the right thing to do. So I told Mum and Dad they were right, I would return to full-time education, with their financial support to an 'adult environment'. In hindsight I am sure Adrian had been coerced and bribed by my father with cigarettes!

To my complete amazement the three years at the FE, full name Hastings College of Further Education, were the most fantastic three years of 'growing up' and social development any teenager could wish for. I learnt to appreciate real ale, play racket sports, lost my virginity to a rampant Corsican nymphomaniac, matured and widened my vocabulary of four-letter words, learnt to appreciate blues and rock music and listened to albums night and day. I made loads of new friends and discovered a sense of humour, shaped by my peers and Monty Python. In essence I learnt to enjoy life. Of course I did not have a care in the world. I lived at home with Mum and Dad and a sister who wouldn't talk to me, and one who wouldn't shut up.

I did not know what responsibility was, let alone the meaning of career, family, mortgage and the drudgery of life. I had not imagined the positive benefits of any of these extracurricular activities of college life when I reluctantly enrolled at the FE in September 1974 at the grand old age of seventeen.

To my absolute surprise students didn't beat each other up, took the tutorials seriously, nobody was disruptive and we enjoyed our chosen subjects. It dawned on me slowly we were all there on a voluntary basis and therefore rebellion and revolution was pointless. As one tutor so subtly put it: 'I assume you are here because you want to be here, so if you don't like it you can piss off right now.' Charming and straight to the point, I appreciated that – good on him.

The lecturers generally were in a different class to my former school teachers. The vast majority were far more academic; although free from pupil harassment were inevitably much more relaxed and often shared benign humour with the students. A Mr Woodlodge was a lovely old chap in his sixties with an interesting history in manufacturing industry management and academia. He dressed like a Harvard professor, in a sports jacket and flannelled trousers. His moustache, above his top lip, was the same size and shape as his little red bow tie. He taught a variety of subjects not on the Grove School curriculum such as English language, arithmetic and economics. He had a tremendous ability to relate to his students and never ever patronised them.

I discovered a whole new circle of friends of similar age and lack of educational opportunity. These years (1974–77) at FE coincided with that of Stevie Elder of Bexhill, and the 'Reverend' Marcus Ball, who resided in Rye. My father coined the name 'Reverend' as Marcus had a tendency to sit with his hands clasped in front of him, as if in prayer. He was also extremely well spoken as if from public school, which he wasn't.

'Reverend' suited him perfectly and it stuck. He considered himself to be the college sex symbol, tall and broad, a smile the girls loved and flashing white teeth. Immaculately well-groomed, his dress sense was nevertheless a bit offbeat. I felt he was perpetually a couple of years behind the fashion scene, not that many FE students set the pace when came to flared trousers, wide collars and velvet jackets and those ludicrous platformed shoes. Personally I was happy in my Levi's, T-shirt and or sweatshirt.

On one occasion a female lecturer in English Literature, one Mrs Dougherty cornered Marcus and myself and suggested we might like to date her daughter, who she told us was about our age and 'needed to be taken out'. This put us in a very awkward position as Marcus rightly expressed – to me, not Mrs Dougherty – if she is pretty we might end up wanting to shag her, alternatively if she turned out to be a right old cow it could be more than a little embarrassing! Either way we would be compromised. I politely explained to Mrs D that our girlfriends probably would not be too pleased if we took Miss Dougherty Junior out, so gracefully declined. It was a kind of white lie, which seemed to do the trick and afford us the perfect escape route.

Steve Elder was about as straight-laced as you could get; he always wore the same dark clothes whatever the season, whatever the weather. He was not a particularly original thinker, but could be extremely funny and was quick with one-line quips. He was however an exceedingly sociable bloke with a good eye for the crumpet, with occasional success. He enjoyed participating in all the ridiculous antics our little gang got up to, whether competing on the tennis court, the pub crawls or just the banter, practical jokes and womanising.

I suspected Hastings FE was the first freedom he had enjoyed away from his dominating mother. His desire to hitchhike around the States with Marcus Ball was one hell of a break for real freedom.

Another good friend was Gerald deBoulle, known as 'Golden Bollocks', son of a local infants' school headmistress from Guernsey and a career civil servant from the Sunderland. Smooth talking and good looking, with a fast wit – quite what he was doing sitting 'A' levels at the age of nineteen, Lord alone knows. Gerald hated the epithet 'Golden Bollocks', which of course only made it worse for him. However, after a year or so it somehow got abbreviated to 'Golden' which he rejoiced in, but not by me I might add. He took pride in his 'French' surname and wondered out loud if he had Norman heritage. I pointed out to him that the Normans were the invaders and us Anglo-Saxon locals still held a grudge against the French. He also seemed to miss the point that as his father was from Wearside it wasn't that likely he had Norman ancestry, especially after nine hundred years. This didn't bother deBoulle one bit, as academically he was streets ahead of everyone and he knew it. He should have been at university, not a college of further education. Gerald had a fantastically fast wit and wicked sense of humour, could pull a woman at fifty paces and played a mean game of squash. To his credit and to general astonishment of all, he only ever drank Coca-Cola, never smoked and ate peanuts by the bucket full. His wardrobe was generally a bit drab and boring, as for the entire three years we were at the FE he only ever wore plain trousers or Wrangler jeans, boring striped shirts and/or round-neck woollen pullovers as though he was a business executive on a casual weekend off. Gerald's other claim to fame was he was the only student in our circle to own a car, a fifteen-year-old Wolseley Hornet. This had great attraction to the girls and to most of the blokes too as a free taxi ride.

Then there was Jimmy the Greek, destined to serve tea and baked beans in the family 'greasy spoon business' for the rest of his life. Jimmy was a sharp dresser; he always wore well-pressed flares and slim-fit shirts from Foster Bros and sported a variety of gold chains around his neck, which he changed constantly. I often wondered if he had one for each day of the week. Jimmy liked to spend time sitting in the college library reading newspapers. He devoured news and information like a sponge and always had a view on what was happening in the world. He despised anyone who read the *Sun* or the *Mirror* and was quick to put them down, with comments like 'load of old crap' and 'only a Moran would look at that shit'. There were a lot of pseudo-academic students who hid behind the broadsheets, not least *The Guardian*. I was ridiculed for always gravitating to the *Daily Telegraph* (DT). Tories were much despised at the FE, however what the majority of students didn't appreciate was the DT was by far and away the best sports paper and its cricket coverage was second to none. E W Swanton and Christopher Martin Jenkins were worth the cover price alone.

Silent Sam, who could eat and drink but not speak, seldom seen on the college campus. Sam would follow us into the pub like a phantom, in a huge ex-army surplus great coat which seemed to swamp him, and sat aloof listening to the conversation and banter without ever contributing. However, once he was past the four-pint mark we couldn't shut him up. The trouble was, unlike Jimmy who was as about as right wing as it was possible to be, Sam was a closet Commie. He was definitely in the 'come the revolution man, you will all be put up against a wall and shot' brigade.

Phil the Phallic had cherubic features and blond curls, was born and bred in Hastings, but had this strange obsession with his Scottish ancestry; he was proud of being a local Sussex boy but even prouder of being Scottish, which he palpably was not. Phil also had every Beatles, and Beatles solo album, ever released by the Fab Four, quite a collection. Phil was also a devout Roman Catholic and occasionally made mention of the 'One True God'. His religion was conflicted by his love of women. We were all at a party one time, when Phil had pulled a girl and made to leave early with her, when Golden Bollocks shouted out across the room 'Remember you're a Roman Catholic, Phil', much to everyone's amusement and their eternal embarrassment.

Kieran Boult a spurious destitute aristocrat with an Irish lilt, who I think was on day release from a local institution. Kieran was hyper intelligent and liked to smoke marijuana disguised as John Player No.6. He was weird. He looked like shit; wore crappy old clothes mainly acquired at the local Oxfam shop. He was a sex maniac and had a different girl in tow just about every week. It was a mystery to me how he did it. He had no discernible good looks and was permanently broke. Clearly there had to be something, which was maybe only apparent to all the women he frequently conquered!

Tommy Staines, he of the most unfortunate name and the butt of most practical jokes. Big, burly and muscular and as soft as a cuddly toy, he was a great bloke but not necessarily the brightest at the FE. His inability to read any given situation was legendary. Somebody once strung his moped 20 foot up a tree by its front wheel. He suspected it was a drunken student from the art department next door, who had taken a dislike to Tommy, after Tommy had been seen chatting up his girlfriend. Armed with half a dozen eggs he identified the art student's car, a white Hillman Imp, and smashed the eggs all over it. He did a very professional job covering the windscreen, roof and bonnet with the eggs and left them to bake dry in the warm spring sunshine. Unfortunately for Tommy it was the wrong white Hillman Imp. This one belonged to a bunch of Arabs who went berserk at what they wrongly interpreted to be a racist attack on their property and integrity. Of course they had no way of knowing who had done it, but we sort of

15

hinted that he may know something about it and Tommy wasn't seen in Hastings for a fortnight. Myself, Jimmy and Golden Bollocks felt quite bad about that for a while but never admitted we had shopped him!

The lovely Saffron 'Saffie' Bybrook was an honorary bloke, born and raised in Stoke-on-Trent or as she insisted 'Churnet Valley actually'. She would have never have made the Pirelli calendar, but had great charm and quirky good looks. She spent far more time with us blokes than she did with the other numerous girls at the FE. I genuinely think she loved all the humour, banter and mucking about more than the girlie stuff. Her dress was more masculine than not and rarely was seen without her trusty faded Levi's. She could also whack a tennis ball harder and faster than Billie Jean King. Saffie was a real 'Tomboy' as my mother would say, larking about, drinking and breaking wind with the best of them. She certainly had the hots for Golden Bollocks, although not deBoulle's type at all. I did pull her once after a particularly heavy evening out in Hastings Old Town, but we were total opposites and we both chalked it down to an erroneous inebriated experience.

Mick Hurst who always wore battered a black leather jacket and rode a BSA Bantam 175cc motorbike, which was perpetually covered in mud as if he had been rallying; maybe he had, I don't know. Mick was only about 5'5" and very thin. He often came to college in 1960's-style bell-bottom strides. He only had a 26-inch waist and the bottom of his bell bottom trousers were the same width. We pondered if he could wear them upside down! Arguably he looked puny, which may explain why the leather jacket never came off, but he had an unbelievable capacity to sink pints of beer. Saffie called him 'Hurst the Thirst'. Mick was proud of his nickname and played up to it at any opportunity. Jimmy once called him 'Mick the Prick' and regretted it!

Black Henry Smith (who was white), real name Brian Smith, the son of a village publican and squash player supreme. 'Black Henry' loved gangster movies and picked his ridiculous nickname up from a TV gangster character. He once told us a cracking story that happened to him when he was fifteen or sixteen. He was involved in an accident, which resulted in his testicles being bruised and swollen. He was admitted to hospital where a nurse had to apply a gel or cream to his injured parts every six hours. To be fair to the young lad, the hospital allocated the fattest and ugliest nurse they could find – a real old battle axe – to administer the treatment and rub it in. To Brian's eternal embarrassment he could not suppress a rock-hard erection each time. He didn't know where to look, but there was no telling where the ugly sister was looking. I always admired him for having the courage to tell this story against himself. It took balls, black or otherwise, and he seemed to dine out on it quite a bit.

James 'Jamie' Hermarnus – or Humongous as he was called – was a great bloke, small in stature and mad in head, with demonic eyes, Jamie was technically part of the art department next door, where he was taking a diploma in Exhibition and Museum Design. Generally the students of the art department and those of the mainstream college didn't have the opportunity to mix that much. However, we would often meet in the refectory for coffee at odd times and share the latest college gossip and scandal like a couple of old women. Hot tottie was normally high up the agenda. Jamie was a fitness fanatic. He would normally run five or six miles before coming to college. He spent his weekends at athletic meetings and competing in long-distance running events. His family life seemed a little complex; I believe he lived with an aunt, but twice week met his mother, who must have lived locally, at a tea room in Hastings Old Town called the 'Horse's Nose Bag'. Most of the gang found the concept of the Horse's Nose Bag quite comical, but no one wanted to offend Jamie as he clearly had a tough time. Unfortunately, I never met Jamie outside of college, which was a shame. He was great company.

Finally there was Julian 'JJ' Eaton-Rye, whom I had known since we were both seven years old. JJ was a bit like the school swat. Always buried in books and seemed to think his education was more important than enjoying himself, a concept completely alien to 99% of all known students. His musical tastes were influenced by a much older brother – who in turn influenced mine – we were totally aligned when it came to John Mayall, the Rolling Stones, Bob Dylan, Neil Young, Eric Clapton/Cream, Led Zepp and Genesis and most good rock bands. We would be forever listening and swapping albums through our adolescence. Julian was quite intolerant of what he considered to be manufactured pop and didn't take too much notice of the 'Hit Parade' in his youth, especially when the John Mayall's Blues Breakers was bringing out a new album on the Decca label. No comparison!

Anyhow these blokes and blokesses were my mates in the period 1974–1977. We grew up together and we had the time of our lives. Over the three years we spent together at the FE we became inseparable as a strong bond grew between us all. We were an odd eclectic mix of individuals with the common theme of catching up on our lost education, playing sport, a fairly hard drinking culture, but most of all embracing life and loving every minute of it against a background of amusing tutorials, banter and piss taking, the blues, rock 'n' roll and sex sex sex! Girlfriends came and went a bit like a revolving door, our 'mates culture' trumped everything and to be honest that drove most of the girlfriends away.

Summer 1977 would be pretty much like the summers of 1975 and 1976, sponge off the state – with no intention of seeking employment. The idea of being paid while not working was very appealing. My only fear was my father finding out his son was drawing the dole as I am quite sure he would have killed me. My view was 'more fool the government for letting me get away with it'. The summers were spent lounging on the beach of Hastings or St Leonards and drinking beer at the taxpayers' expense. The sun always shone bright and hot and the beer always tasted like Double Diamond, fizzy, warm and horrible. More often than not it *was* Double Diamond – fizzy, warm and horrible.

Alternatively I would watch County Cricket at Hove. Sussex's big two star players were Tony Greig, the England captain and swashbuckling all-rounder, and John Snow, England's premier fast bowler and by far the best of his generation. When they turned it on they were an absolute joy to watch. However, Sussex didn't win much with them; without them they were absolute duffers. In 1975 Sussex lost eight consecutive County Championship matches, thirteen in all and was damned lucky to only finish bottom!

I went to a lot of these games both home and away and can confirm it was bloody hard work watching Sussex, but perversely I absolutely loved it. County cricket conveyed a unique atmosphere and some of the characters at Hove and many other grounds were part of the furniture. Most of the old boys had grown up with Sussex and never seemed to miss a day's play. I felt relaxed and welcome. These characters loved to talk cricket all day long and despite some of the awful performances unfolding on the field of play the County game really got under my skin. I felt destined to grow into one of these regulars myself; I really couldn't think of a better way to spend my spare time, other than actually playing myself.

From early '77 I would spend time with the beautiful Jayne on her parents' farm in rural Sussex, on the edge of the South Downs. I had met Jayne at a barn dance at Lewes can you believe! I was infatuated with her from the first time I clapped eyes on her. She wore a red floral dress which revealed more than she intended. Jayne was beautiful in a non-classical way, of medium build and height (a little chunky) with dark wavy hair disguising her beautiful curves and magnificent broad shoulders. A farmer's daughter, she generally tended to dress as though she was ready to milk a cow or turn over the sods, in sensible land clothes and Wellington boots. Whatever she wore she was extremely sexy in my eyes and extremely desirable. I was a problem for her, as she made it clear her wedding night would be the first time for her, which left me in a frustrating sexual vacuum. She rightly felt I was not committed to her as she said cricket and drinking were more of a pleasure to me than she was. As much as that stung, I couldn't disagree. The Hastings FE drinking 'mates culture' was a major part of my life then and Sussex cricket held a fascination for me which was hard to explain, but I just loved being around the professional game. I certainly wasn't anywhere near ready for any sort of normality or commitment, marriage or settling down. I wouldn't have known what it was. I was torn, as I had really fallen for Jayne. I was twenty years old, kind of free and looking to explore the world. The relationship had 'doomed' written all over it and by September Jayne ended it as she felt we had drifted too far apart. It hurt, but I knew she was right.

I also knew this would be the last of three such summers, having completed three fairly ineffectual academic years of further education at Hastings College. In my case the word 'further' was superfluous. College *was* my only serious education. Academically I was still pretty hopeless, I passed a few 'O' and 'A' levels, which made my mum and dad feel good about me, but meant little to me as Environmental Technology, Sociology and Economic History were never going to feature significantly in my future life. But as an education in life it was second to none. It really was the University of Life – I had developed from teenager to young man, still very immature and green behind the ears, but I felt I could take on the world, if only I could find my passage out of Hastings.

As August gave way to September '77 it started to dawn on me life would be different in the future. I had absolutely no idea what I wanted to do with my life, other than continue to have a good time. University education was not an option and it was never something that I had ever seriously considered. 'A' level grade Cs and Ds would only get me into the South Bank Poly and even I knew better than that. It was not for me, the grades reflected my lack of effort at tutorials. I did actually enjoy the educational aspect of the FE, but the social, sexual and drinking side completely dominated. So I figured against all my better instincts, I had better look for some sort of work, especially as the DHSS was starting to rumble me.

As luck would have it I saw a job advertised, 'To assist the van driver with deliveries of furniture' for

Debenhams. I put on my best Montague Burton's green checked suit and spotted tie and went to the interview. They thought I was a little overdressed but gave me the job all the same – guaranteed to Christmas. I think I was the only prat to apply. Forty quid a week plus tips. After £14.50 on the dole I thought this was not at all bad. I worked alongside a wrinkled old workhorse called Benny Jackson. Benny always dressed like Charlie Drake in those window-cleaner sketches, his thinning hair somehow clung to the rungs between his many creases, which amused me no end. 'Saves combing it' was his only comment. Benny was fantastic at extracting money from Debenhams clients. He would concoct a list of affordable charges to take unwanted items of furniture away, this could include anything from old beds and mattresses, to dining tables, armchairs and sofas to sideboards and wardrobes. We would take all the old crap to one of several second-hand furniture shops in Hastings and sell it on to them at the best price we could agree. Benny always split the takings with me fifty-fifty. He was the salt of the earth that bloke.

2. Blood Sucking Mosquitoes And The Man-Eating Dog

Contemplating this involuntary change of lifestyle over a pint in Hastings Old Town one night with Gerald Golden Bollocks (on Coke), he told me that the Reverend Marcus Ball had returned from Canada, indeed had been back for some weeks, and was on his way to the 'Pump House' to tell us all about his travels. After an hour or so the door crashed open and in strode Marcus, hair down his back, face deeply tanned and white teeth glowing and grinning in triumph.

'Hello chaps! I've just jetted in from Vancouver,' he announced.

'No you haven't, Marcus,' says I. 'You have just flown back from Vancouver; don't be so bloody pretentious. So what have you done with Stevie?'

'Ah Steve is still somewhere in British Columbia, at least he was a few weeks ago. I had to come home, my mother was not at all well.'

Somehow this didn't surprise me, I really couldn't see Marcus lasting the course, but I was very impressed that Stevie was still out there somewhere thumbing his way across the Americas.

'And you just upped and left him? How is your mum? Are you going back out there to catch up with Steve?'

'No I'm not and Mater is much better thank you,' said Marcus, 'I have got a job in the City with a major investment bank. Starting next week.'

'Christ, are you sure?' asked Golden Bollocks.

'You've only got one A level grade C in Sociology.'

'Oh yes a really good friend of my father is a city big wig and has arranged it all.'

'Fucking hell, Ball, you're a jammy bugger. Are you sure you're not there just to make the tea? Have they interviewed you yet?'

'Oh yes, went up to the "Smoke" Tuesday of last week. I've got the job.'

'Well that's that then. But what of Stevie? Is he OK?' I asked.

'Yes of course. We met these two American chaps in the Rockies, Guy and Herbie; they were on holiday, ever such nice people, from the West Coast. They invited us to look them up when we got to California. I think Steve was keen to get down the Pacific Highway to spend a few days with them. They were travelling with this other couple and their daughter Rachael from San Diego. I think Steve fancied his chances with her. So I guess that's where he's heading, if he's not there already.'

'So when do think he will come home, Reverend?'

'Absolutely no idea. I suppose when he runs out of money. He might get a job of course; we talked about it. It's easy enough just casual work, cash in hand. Mexicans do it all the time.'

'Have you spoken to Stevie's mum or dad since you returned?' enquired Golden Bollocks.

'I went round to their house the day after I got back. Steve had given me a parcel of stuff to give them.'

'Probably a bundle of dirty washing,' I chipped in.

'No, it was a load of souvenirs and surplus clobber.'

'And?'

'And what?' said Marcus.

'What did you tell them about abandoning their son in Canada?'

'Well nothing really. I just explained about my mother.'

'Oh bollocks, Marcus,' said Gerald deBoulle. 'You just came home at the first chance of a job in the City and used your mum as an excuse to cut it short.'

'No, no, no Stevie fully understood. I left on good terms; no hard feelings.'

'Well does he know you have a job then?' I asked.

'No of course he doesn't I haven't spoken to him in the last three weeks.'

'Some fucking mate,' said Golden Bollocks.

Pondering Marcus and Stevie in Canada and America, at quiet moments during the long dark nights of autumn, it slowly dawned on me that if bloke like Marcus could fly across the Atlantic to the States and hitchhike from one side to the other then why on earth couldn't I? I liked Marcus but he was a bit of a prat. Everyone at college knew he was a little bombastic and a bit arrogant, while at the same time an easy going, happy-go-lucky sort of guy. But as I'd just seen, when it suited him, Marcus came first whatever the circumstances. Maybe it was a slight superiority complex but it was undoubtedly his Achilles heel. The more I thought about it the more I kept thinking 'I could do that.' I was twenty-one and didn't really have the faintest idea of where my life was heading. I didn't have a career path mapped out and wasn't destined for the big time. Deep down it was a concern without an answer. My mind was fogged up and I couldn't see the way forward with any clarity. It didn't help that Dad kept banging on about 'a proper job' and career and saving for a pension. Periodically he would thrust the situations vacant pages in front of me with some God-awful jobs circled in red ink, from working as a clerk in an insurance office or a trainee accountancy apprenticeship to working in the British Rail administration office on Hastings station. I guess there was genuine concern behind his well-intentioned ambition for my future. I wasn't ungrateful and didn't want to go against him, but nothing felt right. Hastings was dragging me down. The one thing I did want was to escape home and Hastings and this wild thought of emulating Marcus and Stevie grew inside my head almost daily. There would be plenty of time for the mundane in the future.

Stevie Elder had quietly returned home sometime before Christmas and had kept his head down. We met up on a normal Saturday night in January 1978 during our weekly ritual old town pub-crawl. Very simply the old town ritual was a drinking route and we all had a fair idea of the time we would be in each pub. Kicking off at 'Mr Cherries' on St Leonards promenade, a modern and somewhat pretentious establishment catering to the young and trendy, 'Piss Elegant' as Kieran described it, seemed to sum it up. We'd walk along the seafront to French's, which was without question the best pub in Hastings; in fact I doubted there was a better pub in the whole of the

UK. With oak panelling throughout, tall panelled columns and five original nineteenth-century Spanish sherry casks displayed ten foot above the bar with spot lighting, it was a classy joint. The clientele was varied, with young and old, business men rubbing shoulders with local council workers, shoppers with students. The place was always crammed full. Along the back wall was a row of about fifteen chairs, these always seemed to be occupied by the more elderly. The big joke amongst us was if one died they would all move up a chair. We called it Death Row.

We would then all move on to the old town; the Anchor (known to all as the Wanker), the Pump House, Hasting's oldest pub with oak beams and low ceiling, 'The First In Last Out' normally referred to as the FILO, the Cinque Ports or the Crown – these were traditionally fisherman's pubs – and finally the Nelson, a fantastic spit-and-sawdust pub, where the local bikers and heavies used to hang out. Often considered a centre for the whacky baccy, pills and white powder, this made it a very intimidating pub to frequent, which is why it was always last – you had to have had a few pints to pluck up the courage to walk through the door. The smell of the marijuana joints hit you as soon as you walked in. Getting high by inhaling second-hand smoke was not so unusual, a bit like going to a Grateful Dead concert! Once inside the Nelson it had a magical atmosphere about it. The pub had just about the best juke box anywhere; it was like my 'wish list' stuffed full of classics by The Allman Brothers, The Who, Peter Green's Fleetwood Mac, Clapton, Supertramp, Jackson Browne, JJ Cale, Steely Dan, Lynyrd Skynyrd etc., etc. No plastic pop in this pub.

Our pub route was well rehearsed, so mates would know roughly where to join up for a pint if they weren't out for the entire night. There was only one rule; you had to drink a minimum of one gallon (eight pints) of real ale. In Gerald deBoulle's case eight Coca-Colas. As a CAMRA member it seemed only right to support them by consuming as much Harveys, Beards, Fremlins, King & Barns and Directors Bitter as possible.

Anyhow, somewhere along our blurred path Stevie was waxing lyrical about the previous four months in Canada and the USA and making me green with envy. Stevie and the Reverend Marcus had left the UK last July and flown to Boston. The reason they chose Boston was partly based on price and the fact that Marcus had a cousin who lived on Nantucket Sound, Cape Cod, who put them up for a few nights.

'So seriously, Steve, where exactly did you go and what was it like on the road?'

'How long you got, mate?' he replied.

'Come on, just give an overview.'

'Well once we left Boston we pretty much headed in a straight line due west, taking us through Syracuse, south of Niagara, then right on along the south shoreline of Lake Erie.'

'Where's that? I've never heard of it.'

'Between the States and Canada. You won't have heard of half the places we went through. We were following the map just heading west the whole time, well nearly, but we'll come to that. Spent a couple of days in Cleveland – that's Ohio – skipped Detroit as the Reverend didn't fancy it and went straight on to

Chicago, you know, Al Capone and all that. Great place Chicago, well worth a visit. Marcus pulled a couple of women there. Girls were all over him, they thought he was fucking Tom Jones or David Cassidy or God knows who! These girls dragged us down to their university campus at the place called Champagne, Illinois. Classic American college just like you see at the movies.'

'So what is so special about Chicago?'

'One of the largest cities in the States has everything. Great history. Rich – just your sort of thing – in many ways it reflects the American story. There were museums galore, not that we went to many, but the main thing I picked up was how rapidly the city grew from nowhere in the 1830s. People, immigrants, kept pouring in and many industries developed there. Great feats of engineering saw the State's first sewage system revolutionise the city and make it liveable. Apparently there was a major fire in Chicago which burnt down the best part of the downtown area in about 1870. This gave them licence to build a brand-new city and some of their old architecture is stunning. Marcus couldn't believe it when we stumbled into what was described as the world's first skyscraper, built in 1885 can you believe. Not very tall when compared with the Sears building.'

'What's the Sears building?'

'Only the tallest building in the world.'

'Oh, where's that then?'

'Chicago – dickhead! I did go to one museum; the transport museum. The reason Chicago is so prominent is its location at the top of the Mississippi on Lake Michigan. As the railways grew, Chicago became a major east/west hub. One really interesting thing I learnt at this museum was because there are so many different railway companies and stations, the authorities needed to standardise the time zones across the USA to bring consistency and discipline to the timetable. So the four American time zones were developed specifically to accommodate the railway timetable.'

'How did they set the time before that?'

'Not really sure. I guess each town just set the clock to wherever they liked. The other fascinating thing about Chicago is what they call their "L", the rapid transit system. Unlike our underground or the New York Subway, theirs is elevated above ground and makes one hell of a din. You can see it in the old gangster movies. We went on it just for the hell of it. It was great.'

'You were really into it, weren't you?'

'Yeah, and here's one more obscure fact I learnt, which I bet you don't know – during World War Two, Chicago alone produced more steel than the whole of the UK.'

'Wow.'

'And another piece of useless information I picked up, was the atomic bomb was developed in Chicago.'

'Where did you pitch your tent then?'

'Talk about change of subject! No, we couldn't do that, so we stayed in a youth hostel until Marcus pulled Susie and Hilly and went down to Champagne and shacked up with them for a couple of nights.'

'Did you get your leg over?'

'No the bastard shagged them both, I think. But I

had my success stories along the way.'

'How on earth did they come up with the name like "Champaign"?'

'God knows. Bizarre isn't it. There are loads of towns and places in America with peculiar names. Anyhow, after that we hitched hundreds of miles through fairly boring country which could be both beautiful, rugged and just plain uninteresting such as Des Moines Iowa, North Platte Nebraska, Casper Wyoming, until we got to Denver in Colorado. That was fantastic.'

'Why?'

'Hard to put my finger on it exactly. Like most cities in America it's very modern but also had some notable early 20th-century architecture not least the Union Station and "city hall". The city is reputedly about one a mile above sea level. Visitors often can't cope with the thin air and suffer from what they call altitude sickness.'

'Were you and Marcus alright?'

'Yep, didn't seem to affect us. Denver is situated on what they call the "High Plains" and subject to a lot of different weather conditions. The only thing for us was it rained most of the time and was stinking hot, but I did like it. It couldn't have been more different to Chicago.

'From there we went on to Salt Lake City, which was alright, but probably wouldn't go back. We got a lift with a Canadian guy called Andy who effectively talked us into going up to Canada. He lived in Edmonton and was heading back home. We got on really well with him, he was a bit far out, but quite British in terms of his humour and we could really relate to each other. We stayed with Andy at his house for a few days. He was a civil engineer of some description; didn't really understand what he did. What he did do was a real "sales" job on the Rockies and told us we would be mad not to see them. So we decided to change direction and head north with him. Suffice to say the Rockies were all he said they were and more, and we met loads of interesting people there at the campsites and bars. However, it was at this point the Reverend Marcus started talking about coming home. We had a real row about it. He gave me some guff about his mum being ill, which I didn't really believe, but within a week he caught a coach to Vancouver and flew home. I flatly refused to come with him. I was enjoying it too much. By then we had met up with some guys from California – Guy and Herbie and Tim and Debbie and their beautiful daughter Rachael at a place called Banff. They lived down at Redlands just south of LA and were to become good friends. You pretty much know the rest from Marcus.'

'Honestly Steve you make it sound fantastic, I can't tell you how envious I feel, I really admire you for having the balls to go through with it and actually pull it off. When you first spoke about it last year at college I thought the whole thing was just a fantasy "pie in the sky" dream. I don't suppose you would consider doing it again?'

'Big question, mate, I mean I would love to, but not with the Reverend Marcus Ball. Next time I want to complete the circuit. I only got as far as LA and returned home.'

'Why?'

'Because it gets bloody lonely, boring and gutty on your own. Once Marcus flew back in September, I then had a further two months on my tod. If it wasn't for Herbie and Guy, who by the way turned out to be gay, not that you would know, other than they shared a king-size round double water bed! I stayed with them for two weeks and spent a few days with Rachael, who lives down in San Diego – she's a student there, I would have come back a lot sooner than 16th November.'

'This Rachael, were you playing hide the sausage with her?'

'Not for the want of trying but she had a boyfriend, Kirk, an ice hockey player, built like an outdoor shithouse!'

'So,' I asked, partly emboldened by alcohol and my Hastings blues, 'would you do it again if I came out with you? Do the circuit properly? Complete it?'

'I guess I could, despite the fact you fart a lot,' responded Steve.

'Is that a yes then?'

'Your farting is a very serious consideration, bearing in mind we will have to share a two-man tent most nights.'

'Give me break, I only fart after eight pints,' I argued in my own defence.

'Look seriously, Rich, I wouldn't want to go to all the same places again, if I go back it we would have to take a different route, maybe see more of Canada. I'd be very happy to go to the Rockies and to California again but that's about it. North America is a big place; there is so much to see.'

'So, if we can agree on an alternative route, you'd do it?' I persisted.

Stevie smiled; we shook hands, 'You've got a deal mate.'

Unlike all my mates at the FE, including Marcus and Stevie prior to their departure last summer, I had plenty of experience hitchhiking in the UK. My blind faith in supporting Sussex CCC led to me follow them to away matches in such places as Derby, Gloucester, Northampton, Leeds, Southend, Manchester and Taunton. I hitchhiked to all these venues, sleeping in a tent, more often than not at the ground itself, but always with the permission of the groundsman. Occasionally in the winter I also hitched to Cardiff to see my older sister who had followed some bloke who was at university down there. Plus I had a friend at Liverpool Polytechnic, so hitched up to Merseyside to see him and watch Everton FC and drink copious amount of Higson's beer. I went to see the Beatles Cavern in Matthew Street, but it had been bulldozed and flattened. A minuscule statue with the words to 'Four Boys who Shook the World' was the only evidence that a seismic music revolution had once evolved here. It seemed to me they were unappreciated in their own city.

I never had a problem hitching and normally got to my destination in good time and without any problems. Hitching is all about common sense; I always took the view, hitch like you mean it, stand up straight with a solid arm and look the driver in the eye and look confident. I always found a part of the road where a car could pull in and stop, ideally on a slow part of the road. The other thing I found if on busy roads if there were several other hitchers move away, preferably in front of them, but out of sight. A few years back I went to the start of the M1 at Staples Corner and was startled to see over a hundred people all bunched together hitching and hoping for a lift. They didn't have a chance in hell. They all looked dispirited and half-hearted, some were sitting on the side of the road smoking and eating. Any vehicle that stopped would have been mobbed, therefore no cars were stopping. I knew I didn't have a cat in hell's chance, so I walked back into Hendon, stood by some traffic lights and got a lift in two minutes and drove past a hundred pissed-off looking no-hopers, much to their consternation.

The deal with Stevie was to go to New York and blow with the wind. We had five months to save sufficient money for our airfare, camping gear and £500 spending money, the maximum we were allowed to leave the country with.

Of course I was ecstatic of the thought of going to America and Canada, leaving home, leaving Hastings and actually living a life on completely my own terms. So now fully motivated to work I took any job I could find which would pay a reasonable wage. Fifty quid a week was the best I could get in Hastings. I worked in a pickle factory, manually sifting diced onion and carrot, with an overpowering stench of acidic vinegar. I guess if I go to hell for eternal life it couldn't be any worse than this. Maybe it was the Good Lord above exacting his revenge on me for being a lazy git and stealing from the state during the previous three summers. One day talking to a fellow worker during an afternoon tea break a couple of weeks into this prison sentence, he said, 'Good job this, innit?'

I must have looked surprised. 'Is it?'

'Well yeah, of course. You don't have to use your brain.'

I thought, you haven't got a fucking brain. I resigned at the end of the day. Being a conscientious lad I worked a week's notice.

My next job was a petrol pump attendant; the stench of unrefined diesel was almost as bad as the raw vinegar. Two weeks into the new role it snowed. I couldn't feel my feet for ten days. Then in March there was a petroleum tanker drivers' strike and we could not get hold of supplies of petrol. I spent day after day reading paperbacks. No petrol, no customers. I was bored out of my brain. I just couldn't wait for May and escaping to the US and leave little old Hastings and its narrow-minded, small mentality behind. However, March to May is a long time when the clock is ticking by so slowly, to the point at one stage I thought the battery was dead. Pathetically I had more crap jobs at poor rates, mainly consisting of painting and repairing waiting to bore me senseless through to mid-May.

Gradually the day of departure drew near. Stevie and I had carefully selected our backpacks, sleeping bags, tent, cooking utensils and footwear, a flat box of Izal lavatory paper and of course a box of 140 Sainsbury's

Red Label tea bags. We had saved our maximum allowance of £500 each and had decided the cheapest way to fly to New York was by the new Freddie Laker SkyTrain. £59 outbound.

The great thing about Stevie was we had so much in common. He was great with the banter and we always shared a good laugh. We shared a love of women, the only qualification being they were female and beautiful. We also had a passion for beer and rock music, although he had some strange likes and dislikes, for example he loved Abba, I didn't. However, I could understand him adoring the girls in Abba, they were something else. Stevie wasn't overly keen on the blues, especially John Mayall, who was an idol of mine. If Stevie had a downside it was his complete indifference to cricket. He had no interest in it whatsoever and I couldn't hold any sort of conversation on the subject, but in North America he would be in the majority.

During the final week I spent time with my family, even my younger sister spoke to me. I thrashed my mum at tennis (although in her mid-fifties she still played a good game – but not good enough) and lost to Golden Bollocks on the squash court. I went to Hove to see Sussex one last time. Sussex -v- Middlesex B&H match. Sussex 60 all out in 26 overs. They get higher scores in baseball!

I went on a final old town drinking ritual with Stevie Elder, the Reverend Marcus Ball, Golden Bollocks, Saffie Bybrook, Black Henry, Jimmy the Greek, Tommy Staines, Silent Sam, Hurst the Thirst and Phil the Phallic and little sister Cathy who all of sudden panicked that she may never see me again. The gallon was easily achieved and 'Saturdays' Disco wouldn't let us in.

My father was not at all comfortable with the thought of me hitchhiking around the US. He actually suggested that I should wait until retirement, and then travel the States in comfort. Stuff that, I thought, I am twenty-one years old, I want to go now while I am young, fit and unattached, not when I am old and decrepit and lumped with a load of old geriatrics on a Thomas Cook holiday. No thanks! He had been quite grumpy with me since I told of my plans to escape to the States. I guess he wanted a return on his investment in me over the previous three years and suspected he saw my reckless actions as a slap in the face. Unfortunately I just couldn't make him understand it was something I just had to do.

I knew Mum was worried, she had heard far too many gruesome stories about the States, but she seemed to understand better than Dad. She understood I did have a choice. When Mum and Dad were twenty-one, the world was at war. Dad would have been in North Africa, in the Dessert Rats, and Mum was a nurse at Bristol Royal Infirmary. Life did not give them a choice.

They were born after the Great War, life was frugal and my grandparents instilled good old-fashioned Edwardian values into their children. Life for my generation was a hundred times better. However, I had to live my life on my terms and fulfil a dream. I was decided; I was going. And Stevie Elder was going for the second time in a year.

Mum and Dad supplied me with a list of addresses of obscure relatives they had never met, who at some point in the distant past had moved across the Atlantic to build a new life in Canada or the United States and said they would write to them and let them know I might be calling by.

Tuesday 23rd May 1978. Steve and I arrived by train at Gatwick airport just before midnight. At 4a.m. we were the first in the queue at the Laker ticket desk. We bought our SkyTrain tickets at 9.15a.m. as soon as the office opened. Mission duly accomplished, we returned to our bench and waited for the 2.30p.m. departure. Another seven hours in flight with our knees tucked under our chins and we touched down at John F Kennedy Airport, New York. The immigration officer traded the remains of my half-eaten chicken carcass, in return stamped my passport. 'You're welcome to America, boys,' he bawled.

As this was a 'seat of your pants' no-nonsense budget tour, our £500 had to last forever, hotels were strictly off limits. Consequently we hadn't booked any accommodation in advance and it was getting dark upon arrival. We were somewhat knackered on account of the fact we had only slept two hours in the last thirty-six. So we decided rather than get stuck in some New York suburb and get mugged on our first night we had better sit tight and shove off first thing in the morning. At least the chairs at JFK were more comfortable than Gatwick, even if our first experience of an American hamburger was worse than Wimpy (all mustard and gherkins – disgusting). We crashed out for five hours. We woke at 5a.m. to the haunting saxophone of Gerry Rafferty's 'Baker Street' and bought a cup of coffee. The girl behind the counter wanted to know if we were Australians. She seemed surprised when we told her in our best English accents that we were British. She was even more surprised when we informed her that we had arrived the previous evening and had slept the night in the airport.

'Don't you guys know that JFK has one of the highest mugging rates in New York? Worse than Harlem!' There was no answer to that. We bought a road map of North America and caught a bus downtown.

We arrived at the Central Manhattan bus station – it was absolutely pissing down. We had decided not to stay in New York; we would see it properly when we returned for the flight home. We located the road we needed to hitch upstate and found a bus to take us out of the city. We wound up at a small town called Harriman, somewhere in the depths of New Jersey. The rain was still torrential, we managed to find a secluded field to put our tent up. We never used the word erect, it had too many sexual connotations we couldn't handle. We clambered inside, all damp smelly and steamy. Steve became all philosophical and serious. 'You know,' he said, '£500 each ain't gonna last us long.' It converted to just over $2.35 to the pound so we had a little more than $2300 between us which had to last us as long as possible.

Stevie continued, 'We have to be seriously careful what we spend our money on, absolute essentials only. We pitch our tent for free unless we have no choice, never use public transport like we just did, unless absolutely essential and eat as cheaply as possible. We can live on $3 a day each if we really try. I did last year.'

Now he tells me! 'This is going to be some challenge,' I opinioned.

It was 3.15 in the afternoon. We were forty miles from New York, 3500 miles from home. We were bored, wet, hungry and completely knackered. We played cards to pass the time. It was now 6.15.

'Stuff this,' says Steve 'I'm going to have a kip.'

We woke in time for breakfast (there wasn't any), it was 8.00a.m. Now that is what I call a good night's sleep. We had acclimatised and were raring to go. It was time to hitch America on $3 a day.

We had decided to head in the general direction of Niagara Falls i.e. north-west. The rain was lighter. We dismantled the tent, which was now three times heavier and it took us ages to fold it into an acceptable size and shape to strap on to a backpack. We had not found any food to buy so we packed our pristine cooking utensils away unused and hit the road. After an hour we got our first lift. It took us to Ithoua, home of Connell University. It struck us it had better facilities than Hastings College of Further Education. They say everything in America is bigger and better, Connell certainly is!

We were directed to a campsite at a place called Taughannock Park. We were now in Pennsylvania, the rain had at last relented and the afternoon was really hotting up. We took advantage of the shower block, changed into shorts and T-shirts, stocked up on food provisions and went for a hike. We found our way to Taughannock Falls, a fairly impressive waterfall of some height and ferocity. Located on one of the Finger Lakes, the legions of mosquitoes had a real liking and thirst for our European blood. We returned to our tent, our arms and legs and neck covered in red bites. Mosquito repellent was something we had not considered and now it was too late.

We made our first attempt at campside cooking. Not a great success, tinned meat with fat, courtesy of 'Dinty Moore' which was to become a twice-weekly staple that filled us up because it was cheap and readily available throughout North America, but had the knack of making you feel you had been better off with pig slurry. It purported to be a beef stew with vegetables, but at least 35% of it was made from additives such as paste, modified starch, salt, sugar, caramel colouring and flavouring. We had a beer or two to try and kill off the effects of our cuisine, sitting by a pathetic campfire akin to a glowing twig, when we heard a noise, a rip and the sound of a furry creature making its getaway. Steve had bought a box of cereal for breakfast. A raccoon had smelt it, found it, eaten it and torn a nylon shoulder bag to shreds in the process. Stevie was particularly incensed that the majority of his Sainsbury's Red Label tea bags had been chewed. A know-all Texan was full of critical platitudes at our loss. All right we were incredibly naïve, but we don't have raccoons patrolling the leafy lanes of Bexhill and St Leonards-on-Sea, East Sussex.

Stevie then remembered this had happened last year in the Rockies – God preserve us – and tied a rope through the straps of the bag containing the remainder of our food, slung it over a branch and hauled up into mid-air, and secured the rope to the main trunk, just like in the Rockies.

'It all comes flooding back now,' said Steve.

'Great,' said I.

The mosquitoes were becoming thirsty again, so we decided to return to the sanctuary of our tent. We stored the backpacks between the flysheet and the inner tent. Placed our boots outside the inner mosquito-net door, zipped up and lay back, only to hear the hum of a mosquito buzzing around the inside of our tent. We were lying on top of our sleeping bags in just our underpants, it was still very hot and humid. We located the torch and located a mosquito, then another, then another and another and, bugger me – bloody hundreds of them.

'Right we have to be ruthless and take out every one of the little sods,' I directed, 'We get them before they get us.'

Having found T-shirts and jeans we set about methodically squashing every mosquito until the chilling hum of the blood-sucking little bastards had been extinguished. After what seemed an hour of slaughter we clambered into our sleeping bags for a peaceful night's sleep.

The next morning we awoke with the sun silhouetting every squashed corpse on the tent. To our horror virtually every one we squashed left a red stain. Blood. Our blood. There had to be over a hundred stains, a souvenir that would travel around with us for the next six months. We both looked as though we had caught a bad dose of chickenpox. We felt under the circumstances a shower might be in order, on the basis a blood transfusion was out of the question!

A couple of years earlier a mate of mine, Nev Northville, who was the son of my Aunt Val's best friend, had immigrated to Toronto, Canada. Via my Aunt Val, I had contacted the Northville family who had told me if I make it to Ontario I should look then up and stay a few nights. We were now no more than a day or two away from Niagara Falls and thereby Toronto. So Steve and I agreed we would head for Canada to test the validity of the invitation.

It was a bit of a stretch but we attempted to hitch to Niagara in a day. We nearly made it. By 9.30p.m. we arrived in a stifling prairie community by the name of Sanborn, twelve miles short of our target. Being huge open fields of corn, there was just nowhere to conceal a bright green tent. It was getting dark and we were getting thirsty, so we went to the local bar for a beer and to see what might turn up. This was a classical American bar, straight off a film set with a long bar with screwed-down bar stools, pool table, lumberjack shirts, Budweiser and pretzels.

I guess they never had a couple of Brits roll in before. Within ten minutes we'd got a meal, a jug of beer and a garden to pitch our tent for the night.

Her name was Ellen, her husband was a firefighter

but was away fishing some place. She took pity on us and told us, 'You guys can use the back yard. I will have to lock up the dog first.'

Oh shit, I thought. I can't stand dogs, not even little cuddly ones. They always go for me. I guess they just sense I am not comfortable with them.

I always thought a back yard was a concrete square, similar to those you find in back-to-back terrace houses in the north of England. I wasn't sure how we were going to knock the pegs in. But I figured she had to have some grass somewhere.

As it turned out the back yard was a huge very British-style back garden with mature trees, flowerbeds and borders, a small pond and a dog kennel you could keep a pony in. You had to see the dog to believe it. Let's just say it was huge, masculine with a mouth full of sharks' teeth and emitted a horrible growl and dribble. Ellen introduced us to the beast through the galvanised wire mesh door, bolted, chained and locked. It got our scent (not difficult, we must have smelt something awful). This satisfied the monstrous dog and to our amazement settled down and went to sleep.

'He'll be fine now he knows you,' said Ellen. 'But we will keep him locked in tonight – just in case.' Thank God for that, I thought quite sincerely.

The next morning Ellen greeted us cheerily with a mug of tea.

'I guess you guys aren't a couple of junior Jack the Rippers after all. The shower is inside, second on the left, and breakfast will be in forty minutes in the kitchen.'

Adopting our best British manners and trying our best not to look too slovenly we appeared in the kitchen exactly forty minutes later. Sitting at the table was Ellen jnr, aged nineteen and looking absolutely ravishing with her porcelain skin and good looks. Clearly not backward at coming forward, she told us her bedroom overlooked the back yard – there's that strange expression again. She had got out of bed totally naked and drawn back the curtains to see a bright green tent and two fellas rolling up their sleeping bags.

'I jumped back pretty damned quick,' she said, 'and lost my balance on the corner of the bed and crumpled onto the carpet.'

I looked at Stevie. Stevie looked at me. We both looked at Ellen jnr. Ellen snr looked at all three of us. 'Breakfast is served,' she said. A superb fare consisting of a typical American breakfast, including pancakes with maple syrup and bacon, toasted Rye bread and jams, cereals, fresh fruit and coffee. Not only the first real food we had tasted but arguably the best quality food we could have asked for. No Dinty Moore in this household.

We held a bit of a discussion of how to spend today, we knew we had to meet an old friend of mine at 4p.m. over the Canadian border and pondered if we should go via Buffalo en route to Niagara. Both mother and daughter looked at us as though we had taken leave of our senses.

'Why on earth would you want to go there?' asked Ellen senior.

'It's the pits,' chipped in Ellen junior.

'What's wrong with it?' I asked.

'How long have ya got?' came the response in unison. 'It's a rundown industrial city with just about the largest rail hub in the north-west states. It was a real progressive place way back when, but it never recovered from the depression back in the thirties. Frankly it has nothing going for it, the place is a dive, you'd be much better off going straight to the falls; they're fantastic.'

With a recommendation like that we decided to skip Buffalo.

'I'll drive you guys to Niagara if you want,' said Ellen jnr. She did not have to ask twice. We bid our thanks to Mummy Ellen, avoided the man-eating dog and made a dash for the front passenger seat. I sat in the back.

3.   Wobble Wobble And The Wawa Woman

The Niagara Falls were awesome. Spanning the Niagara River on the border between New York State and Ontario they were a sight to behold. There were three falls in total but the largest by far was the Horseshoe Falls, spilling a small matter of six million cubic feet of water per minute over its 160-foot vertical drop. Indeed Niagara Falls has the most powerful flow rate in the whole of North America. The power of the falls was incredibly intimidating as was the spray carried in the winds which drenched us standing on the viewing platform a good quarter of a mile back. Way back in the 1920s some idiot decided to go over the falls in a wooden beer barrel, one can only wonder why. Personally I think he was a looney. As the falls attract millions of visitors from across the globe each year, the balance between tourism and the more industrial and commercial uses, not least hydroelectric power, was an ongoing challenge for the authorities. We got talking to a Falls Tourist Office girl who said 'if you think this is impressive you should see the Iguasa Falls on the border between Brazil and Argentina, they are ten time longer and have over 200 separate cascades.' This was all very interesting but as Stevie pointed out she was meant to be promoting Niagara not the competition!

We had agreed to meet Neville Northville, formerly of Pimlico on the Canadian side of Niagara at 4p.m. It had been five years since I last saw Nev – never Neville – and family. He was now twenty years old and not surprisingly had changed somewhat. The change I had not expected was for him to lose his London accent and sound Canadian. After every sentence he said 'Eh'. I don't know why, just a bad habit I suppose. Wrong – every Canadian man, boy, woman and girl, young or old, black or white – they all said 'Eh' at the end of each sentence. It seemed incredible to me how the entire nation could pick up such an awful habit!

We were to stay with Nev and his folks for a few nights. His mum and dad were Joan and Jim. How they could call their first-born Neville with a surname of Northville was one to ponder. As it turned out, Jim particularly had a wonderful British sense of humour. Things were starting to fall into place. Nev's little sister was no longer so little. Francesca was a little cracker of eighteen and like my kid sister was not really on talking terms with her brother, which made conversation a little strained to start with. However, Jim was a real live wire and was cracking jokes from the moment we arrived.

That evening the entire family was going to the Annual Toronto Darts League Dinner Dance. Steve and I could go too but we had to wear a suit. Oddly enough we had forgotten to pack a suit, so arrangements had to be made. Steve was more Nev's size and jacket, trousers, black shoes and necktie all fitted pretty well. Now me, Richard, I have always been bit on the big side. Jim was bigger than his son, but I was still bigger than Jim. Fortunately I had brought a pair of casual trousers that we felt I might just get away with. A reasonable fitting shirt was found but the jacket was a problem. The situation was resolved when Jim borrowed from his neighbour a sports jacket. It was a loud, garish lime-green, tangerine and purple checked jacket with double lapels stretching out right across the shoulders and two sizes too big! If it had been a fancy dress party I would have backed myself for first prize. But to everyone's amusement, not least Steve, Jim and Joan thought it acceptable, so off we went.

I guess the Canadians do not play darts. The dinner dance consisted of one hundred and fifty Brits. It was just like any private function back home; except they had a rock 'n' roll disco and Labetts beer. The stand-up comedian was straight out of a Geordie Working Man's Club: just priceless. Jim had set his stall out to get myself and Steve well and truly tanked up. Suffice to say we did not need any encouragement despite the gassy lager beer. Friends of the Northvilles came up to me with regular words of sarcasm regarding my appearance. I was at first very polite in an embarrassed sort of way, as to be fair most of the gathering had made a real effort and looked dressed for a wedding. But when one bloke offered me a bunch of balloons he had acquired, I think my second word ended in two 'fs'. It was at this point I realised Jim had set me up by organising a whole procession of people to either sympathise or patronise me all night long. I walked across the ballroom to confront him.

'You know, Richard,' he said, 'I watched you cross the room and I have to tell you, you went the long way round to get here.'

'Whatz do ya mean?'

'Well you did a large semi-circle, like a half moon.'

'You set me up, you bugger,' I slurred, 'people have been taking the piss out of me all night long, they wanna to know if I am dressed like this for a bet,' I drawled.

'Never mind, Richie, we are going home soon, so you can sleep away your sorrow and distress.'

I woke the next morning somewhere around midday with a thumping head. Recovering slowly I watched TV with Steve when we came to the weather forecast. This particular forecast broadcast out of Buffalo for the USA. A guy in faded blue jeans, a red sweatshirt and a blue baseball cap appeared with a huge map of the US. This was equally divided into three, by two straight vertical lines running north to south. In section one: the west it said 'Very Hot'. Section two: middle 'Lots of Rain' and in the third section: east 'Rain Here Too'. Steve and I absolutely cracked up at this child-like amateurish forecast and at the so-called presenter, who slapped his knee, bent double with laughter and failed to enhance his message with any further atmospheric detail such as the rain patterns, high or low pressure areas or isobars. We had never seen anything like it before. Back home we were used to the BBC and Bert Ford dressed in a sombre three-piece tweed suit, starched collar and plain knitted tie. Bert was dull and uninteresting, but always dependable as he would methodically break down the British Isles into regional sections and clearly predict the varied weather fronts and depressions, if not necessarily accurately. He at least had an illusion of sincerity. We thought the weather man from Buffalo was the funniest thing we had ever seen. Joan came into her living room to find two lads convulsed with hysterical laughter rolling around her living room floor. After five years she had been corrupted by American TV and did not see the funny side of it at all. She threw us out of the house for the afternoon.

On Friday 2nd June 1978 I was forced to eat 'foreign' food for the first time in my life. We'd been out all day with Nev and his friend Danny and we had not eaten a thing. As Jim and Joan were out, Danny suggested we send out for a large pizza. I had heard of pizza and knew it was some sort of Italian thing, which no right-thinking English man would take seriously. As it happened, both Danny and Stevie had Italian blood in their veins. Nev loved a pizza, so the decision was quick and swift. I had not said a thing but Steve Elder knew of my discomfort, he understood my reluctance to eat anything other than good old British home-cooking, which he was quick to exploit as soon as the thing arrived.

'Let me cut you a nice big slice, Rich.'

Everyone ate their fill, as I unenthusiastically and squeamishly nibbled round the edge. After ten minutes of this, Danny noticed I wasn't making a pig of myself and deducted I didn't like pizza. I had reached a crossroads. I was starving hungry; it was pizza or nothing at all. Danny was coming for my dinner.

'Leave off, Danny, I'm going to eat this,' I said with a fortitude I was unaware I possessed. I ate it. I quite liked it.

'Christ that was quite good,' I said with total surprise.

Steve then set about explaining the Richard Wynter mentality when it came to 'foreign' foods.

My parents were brought up with coupons, so we ate what we could buy at the butcher's: lamb and pork chops, pig's liver or sheep's hearts, chicken, mincemeat, fish on Fridays and a roast joint on Sundays. My father, who spent too much time in Egypt during the war eating bully beef, looked down upon anything which was not labelled 'Produce of England'. Let's not forget I am my father's son; so it was always meat and three veg. Anything outside of this description was considered by both my father and me as 'foreign rubbish'. It was a bit like the old joke – if you can't spell it or can't stand in it, don't eat it. My parental socialisation shaped and adapted my attitude and my diet. So myself and my sisters were conditioned to believe traditional British food was superior and everything else would be awful, which frankly in 1970's Hastings it was.

Stevie on the other hand is 25% Italian with much younger parents than mine, and as such had a very broad culinary upbringing. As soon as he was off his rusks he was eating Italian spaghetti and pastas, French escargot in garlic, goulash from Hungary, Greek moussaka, couscous from Morocco and curry from God-knows-where.

All this came as somewhat of a surprise to Danny, as living in cosmopolitan Toronto, where anything goes, had never met anyone quite so fussy as me before. He started talking about his vegetarian girlfriend who lived in Ottawa and was trying to draw non-existent comparisons.

I said, 'Isn't Ottawa in Quebec? That's miles away.'

'Oh no, it's not that far, it's about three hundred miles north-east of here but takes five hours to drive, but it is still in Ontario.'

'Christ I didn't appreciate the size of Ontario.'

Stevie said, 'Danny is a proper Canadian and would think nothing of driving for five hours. You have to understand the scales here are about ten times bigger than at home. You could fit the UK into Ontario, no problem, but then again you could fit the UK into most Canadian provinces.'

Changing the subject, Steve asked wasn't it difficult having a girlfriend so far away. Again Danny dismissed the notion of distance and just said she went there to work in the National Gallery of Canada, one of the largest art museums in the whole of North America.

'It's what she wants to do. She loves it there. She comes home some weeks and I go up there, it's no big deal.'

I thought travelling forty miles to see Jayne on her farm north of Burgess Hill was some distance. We let the subject drop.

We spent four to five days in and around Toronto. It had a fairly British climate but with more extremes. Occasionally the summers can approach a whopping 100F and the winters as low as minus twenty. I suspected the summers were more settled and reliable, and the winters bloody hard work! The city had a good blend of old and new and incredibly cosmopolitan in so much as it was a real mix of nationalities and races. Toronto is in fact the second largest Canadian city by population after Montreal and is a magnet for business, finance, the arts, culture and music. You couldn't move for museums, which seemed to be everywhere, housing everything from indigenous Indian relics to military, modern art and fashion.

Unbeknown to me the original settlement was founded by the British and called the City of York from 1793–1834 when the name changed to Toronto. The Battle of York in 1812 saw the Yanks burn down the Parliament building, so the British Canadians responded by attacking the seat of Government, Washington DC. Nice!

We walked all over the place. Everything we went to or saw was supposedly the largest in the world: the largest cinema screen, the largest shopping precinct 'Square One'. The CN Tower the largest free-standing building in the world was hugely impressive, not least its external rocket lift with an all-glass frontage so you can see the ground recede as you are propelled from ground level to top in twenty seconds. The view from the top was outstanding. We also went to Centre Island and Lake Ontario and a dozen other attractions, including a baseball match at the Toronto Blue Jays. This was an interesting experience, very much poor man's cricket. It lacks the skill and grace of God's own sport but makes up for it in speed and passion.

Returning from the game with Stevie, Nev and Jim to Joan's true Canadian dinner, steak followed by blueberry jelly. She had really pulled the stops out, it was wonderful. We'd all had a few beers and were in a buoyant mood, which seemed to wind Joan up. Things came to a head when she served the blueberry jelly, as Jim kept thumping the table with the palm of his hand making the jelly wobble.

'Look Joan it's like your tummy. Wobble wobble,' cried Jim.

Steve and I couldn't help it, we were shaking with laughter. Nev and Francesca knew better. Joan was looking daggers at us.

Jim did it again. 'Joan look, there goes your tummy again. Wobble wobble.' Joan threw a pot at Jim which smashed into the wall.

This was too much; I had to leave the room. Jim had clearly humiliated his wife for our entertainment, while Nev and Francesca just sat there in disbelief.

I felt, although the jelly incident was not of our making, we had probably outstayed our welcome and it was time to move on. Despite pleas from one and all to stay as long as we liked, a week had come and gone, the Northville's generosity had been overwhelming and irresistible, they would not let us spend a cent of our own money. But Canada was a big place and we had a further four provinces yet to discover, so we bade our thanks and hit the road.

On local advice we decided to visit Algonquin Provisional Park. Algonquin was an area of large natural lakes, surrounded by pine forests. It took us all day to hitch there. Our fourth and final lift was in a police patrol car. Canadian and indeed American police cars are full-sized gas guzzlers more than twice the size of the little Morris police vehicles that potter round the streets of Hastings and St Leonards. Hastings' police actually drove Ford Anglias in the 1960s The multi-coloured flashing lights stretched across the top of the car, by contrast to the single spinning blue light back home only replicated by Dr Who's Tardis. The cops themselves all seemed to come out of the same mould, about 6'3" and bulky, broad shouldered and walking with a swagger. Of course the biggest difference was every one of them carried a firearm, which in my view did seem a bit superfluous out here in the wilds of Algonquin Park.

On Tuesday 6th June we hired a canoe and bought a camping permit for four nights and merrily set off on our way in our two-man canoe complete with backpacks and food provisions to last us the four days. We probably canoed about fifteen miles around the lakes. The following day fate took a hand and, due to a navigational error i.e. failure to correctly interpret a simple map, we totally lost our bearing and rowed across a massive lake about two-and-a-half miles wide. We decided to try and backtrack on ourselves, but halfway back across the lake the wind blew up and the water became quite choppy. We spotted a small island no more than 50 x 20 yards. The weather closed in, visibility was poor, the fine penetrating rain had turned into heavy penetrating rain and was pouring down and the temperature dipped to something like 48 Fahrenheit at best. We hauled up the canoe, assembled the tent in double-quick time, made a fire and opened a tin of the delicious *(sic)* Dinty Moore beef stew. We stayed put for twenty-four hours in an attempt to let the rain subside. It didn't. Boredom set in quite fast and we reverted to playing 'Eye-Spy' which is not easy on an island smaller than our back garden back home with zero visibility. After a couple of rounds we gave up and had a go at 'Twenty Questions'. That came to an abrupt end when I had Julie Andrews as my imaginary character. Elder hit me!

We still had light sporadic rain but the wind had eased a bit and we could make out the horizon so we made a dash for it and canoed back to the Canoe Centre which we duly achieved after six hours of hard rowing. It was a shame to have to abandon our time on the lakes, as the scenery was truly breathtaking – or so we were told.

While we were sheltering from the inclement weather, Steve and I decided to review our travel plans and agreed to attempt to hitch the entire length of the Trans Canadian Highway, Canada's Highway 1, all the way to Vancouver and on to Vancouver Island. We had been supplied with addresses and phone numbers of various contacts along the route – friends of Joan and Jim, plus the distant relatives of whom we had never previously heard and contacts Steve had made the previous year – so had a variety of people to visit over the next three thousand miles, some of whom were expecting us and some weren't. Most of them had never heard of us. The first major target was Winnipeg in the Province of Manitoba. This was about a thousand miles from where we were currently situated.

We phoned ahead to contact Sam and his wife Beth

in Winnipeg to let them know we would be with them in three or four days hence. Sam was one of three sons of Elsie who is a second cousin of my father and my Aunt Val. Elsie and Val had exchanged letters and Christmas cards since before the Second World War, but had never met. She was very insistent I made contact with her family and introduce myself. The only thing was, I was not too sure she had passed the message on to her three middle-aged sons. However, a thousand miles is a long way on the road when you are thumbing a lift and we broke the journey down into smaller short-term targets. We identified two towns to head for: Sault St Marie and Thunder Bay. If we could accomplish this we would be in Winnipeg in four days tops.

Wrong. After two days we reached our first target, Sault St Marie. Traffic in this part of Ontario was sporadic and it was not unusual to wait at the side of the road for anything up to four hours. Even then we had some odd lifts; a couple of 'freaks' in a hippies 'groovy van' took us a hundred miles. The van was covered in carpet throughout, including the ceiling. The driver's name was Eugene Archer and he was seriously deranged. His mate Jojo was only slightly less demented. Eugene spoke non-stop nonsense about elephants, lampshades, fire escapes and Macedonians. I couldn't make head or tail of what the hell he was on about; I didn't understand a word. For a while I thought we were back in the UK as he drove on the left-hand side of the road as the 'groovy van' drifted and veered across the tarmac making full use of the space available. We were all damned lucky there weren't any other vehicles on the road. Eugene was on a trip from Sudbury to Newberry (these towns really do exist in Canada); he was also on an LSD trip to the mental asylum. Frankly, he scared the shit out of us and we got out at the first opportunity.

Sault St Marie is situated on the USA border with Michigan, but also at the point where three of the main lakes merge, namely Lakes Huron, Michigan and Superior. Although not by any stretch of the imagination would you call Sault St Marie a major border post, it is the only border post for seven hundred miles in either direction if you want to cross over and go to Detroit, Milwaukee or Chicago. Sault St Marie was a very quiet and unassuming town. We didn't see many people about and it struck me as a bit dull and quiet. Maybe given its remote location that wasn't surprising. It was fairly cold and this was June 10th. I imagine the winters here must be really harsh.

Nev had said that in some parts of Canada the winter temperatures can plummet down to forty below. A bad winter's day in Hastings it may go down to minus two or three, plus the wind chill factor off the English Channel could freeze your nuts off, but minus forty was incomprehensible to us.

Well, thank God it's June!

We were getting good at finding secluded locations to pitch the tent, but here in Sault St Marie it seemed to be academic as we effectively pitched camp right in the town centre, close to the banks of the St Mary's River. It could be seen by passing traffic and pedestrians. As it was so docile, subdued and deserted, we confidently left our backpacks inside the tent and went to a bar for a few beers and a burger. The next morning we didn't dismantle the tent until after ten. It was a bit like we weren't there. We didn't exist. Absolutely nobody noticed a bright green tent in the town centre. We moved out and nobody noticed. Regrettably nor did the passing motorists, so we spent another two and half hours without a lift. There was no way we could make Thunder Bay today. A couple of Swedish tourists in an old banger took pity on us and gave us a lift as far as Wawa, where the old banger gave up the ghost and broke down. They said they would try and get the car fixed and if we were still around in the morning would pick us up again. We thanked them but decided to push on.

Unfortunately we were not the only hitchhikers in Wawa. There were at least two other conventional pairs of hitchers and a group of four guys, who looked like 'the wild bunch' who came sauntering up to us to strike up a conversation. I didn't feel comfortable with them around. There was no way anyone would stop with this gang of tossers. They were rugged, dirty and seriously foul-mouthed. One admitted being on the run from the Alberta police. He said his name was 'Stub', had black teeth and shoved out his left hand to reveal a grimy stub where his thumb should have been. Another answered to the name 'Mingo' and looked like a character out of a Clint Eastwood spaghetti western. Frankly Mingo, who had a face like a deformed rhinoceros, had a bit of a pathological manner about him. Steve and I came up with some excuse and headed off the highway and walked into Wawa. With the competition on the side of the road and a gang of mercenaries on the loose we decided to call it a day. After some negotiations the local motel allowed us to pitch our tent in their grounds, providing we bought a meal in their restaurant.

It is universally accepted that English is the first and official language not only of the British, but Canadians and Americans too. We have different accents and dialects, we have our own colloquialisms and slang, we may put the stress on different syllables and use different phraseology, but fundamentally it's the same. That is how we communicate.

Except in Wawa. The old cliché of 'I say tomato you say tomayta' quite literally held true in the Wawa Motel Restaurant. Like most unimaginative North American restaurants the menu consisted of variations of hamburgers and little else. Tomato is mandatory part of a hamburger and although I have nothing against this innocent vegetable I decided on my own variation and asked for a cheeseburger minus all the gherkins, onions, relish, mustard and tomatoes. The waitress was a plain, regular woman of a slightly unappealing nature, lacking in personality and humour, maybe approaching forty, I wasn't sure from which direction.

'OK, I'll have a cheeseburger, with no tomatoes please.'

'No what?'

'Tomatoes.'

'Sorry, no what eh?'

'No tomatoes.'

'I don't get ya.'

'No tomatoes.'

I just got a blank stare back at me as if I was speaking Swahili. I thought I better wise-up and slipped into a quite awful North American accent.

'NO TOMAYTAS EH.'

'Oh you don't want any tomaytas with the cheeseburgers eh.'

By God, I think the woman's grasped it.

'Yes thanks, no tomatoes – and no gherkins, onions, relish or mustard!' She turned on her heel and with no sense of irony or humour she made her way back to the kitchen to deliver my special request.

The cheeseburger was as about as tasteless as the motel décor with its cheap plastic and dour surroundings However, we had kept our side of the agreement and bought a meal, if you could call it that, before returning outside into the freezing cold and our damp smelly tent. The next morning we brushed the ice off the canvass, somehow rolled it up and packed it away and returned to the motel restaurant to buy a breakfast. I don't like pancakes and syrup for breakfast; where did this idea come from? It seems quite alien to me. Hamburger with or without 'tomayta' was out of the question. Sausages, as I understand them, didn't exist, but we could buy a fried egg and toast, with something called grits. Grits turned out to be deep-fried diced potato with onions and tasted very good. Suitably fortified with a hot breakfast and numerous cups of strong coffee, we hit the highway in a determined effort to make Thunder Bay by nightfall. To our astonishment the two pairs of hitchhikers we had seen the day before were still there, although the wild bunch, thank God, had disappeared. We doubted they had secured a lift; more likely had been detained 'in the local law enforcement B&B' as Stevie put it. We were keen to catch a lift before they broke out!

It was so cold; the temperature didn't rise above one degree all day. I was dressed in virtually every item of clothing I had. Vehicles spasmodically came and went, nothing stopped. The other hitchers weren't doing any better – a French-Canadian couple and two American guys from somewhere I had never heard of. They seemed pleasant enough but they were competition, so we decided to wander back into Wawa in search of our Swedish friends and their old banger; if we could find them this would secure a passage out of this God-forsaken shithole en route to Thunder Bay. Sadly they were nowhere to be seen, so back to the highway and take our chances with the others. However, by 6p.m. we couldn't feel our legs from the knees down. The reality hit us; it would be another evening camping in the borders of the Wawa Motel and that God-awful restaurant.

Tuesday 13th June. Having slept surprisingly well, the next day dawned bright and warmer and we both woke up feeling refreshed and re-energised. With renewed enthusiasm and a bloody-minded determination we set off and walked straight into our French-Canadian competitors. They had procured a large round trash-can plastic lid from somewhere.

About two feet in diameter, they had drawn a Lightning Bolt over a large thumb. Underneath they had written 'Thunder Bay or Bust.' I have to say it was brilliant and very effective, as within five minutes they had got a lift. We retrieved the lid from the side of the road, Stevie held it up above his head looking like the Messiah leading his believers to the Promised Land. It must have made God laugh too as fifteen minutes later we were on our way to Thunder Bay. One lift: 300 miles, we were well happy to be out of Wawa. The guy driving the car was quite chatty and we told him we had been trying for a lift since Sunday afternoon. He nonchalantly said he wasn't surprised as Wawa housed the highest security prison in Canada! No question the Good Lord works in mysterious ways. The bin lid did the trick.

Thunder Bay, close to the US state line with Minnesota, situated on the banks of Lake Superior, proved to be very interesting. An old historic town founded by the first beaver trappers, it became an important distribution centre for beaver fur pelts, which were shipped back to Europe to make gentlemen's top hats. We stumbled across an egg farm on the outskirts of town and the owner, an expat called Bill, said he was happy for us to pitch our tent in a corner of his field. It turned out Bill originally came from a place called Swaffam Bulbeck in Cambridgeshire and had a brilliant Pythonesque sense of humour. He was telling us about the winter snowfall, when he went into a dialogue about a very young Beagle puppy his wife had bought at great expense. Apparently one night with the temperature at 20 below, the dog went outside for a squat and while in the classical crouching position just keeled over sideways stone-cold dead from the strain and freezing temperature. To any normal person this was a sad, pathetic story but to two young lads reared on black humour we found this hysterically funny. Of course the farmer knew how to deliver a good yarn, his description and timing was pure comical genius. Bill then moved on to the subject of pants. To the three of us, pants are Y-fronts or men's underwear. Here on the American continent they are trousers. I didn't know this and happened to mention that back in Algonquin Park somebody at the canoe centre had mentioned my wet pants, which I thought was kind of personal, but let it go, as my pants as well as my jeans really were soaking wet from the rain. Now grasping my previous misunderstanding, Bill went into a whole series of pants v trousers fables he had encountered himself. He claimed it had taken him over a year to work out what the hell was going on.

We still had a way to go to reach Winnipeg, which took us a further couple of days to reach.

Winnipeg has to be one of the remotest spots on the planet. It really is in the middle of nowhere and that's official. It may not be the end of the world but I suspect you could see it from there. The nearest major population conglomerates are Toronto 950 miles to the east, Calgary (Alberta) 750 miles to the west and either Minneapolis (Minnesota) 400 miles slightly to the south-east or 800 miles to Denver (Colorado) slightly to the south-west and absolutely nothing whatsoever to the north. If you drive due south out of Winnipeg, via Dakota's Nebraska and

Oklahoma, you have to keep going in a straight line until you hit Dallas, Texas to see any sizable populous. And yet here in prairie land was this wonderful secluded city, the capital of Manitoba, which stood out like a beacon of humanity – we could have been in Croydon (England) or Perth (Australia) or even Milwaukee (USA). A modern medium-sized town with everything you could wish for set right in the middle of Canada – just as far as it could be from Newfoundland to the east as it would be to Vancouver Island in the west.

Here Stevie and I knocked on the door of an obscure distant cousin Sam on my father's side – who until a couple of months before probably did not know of my existence – and his wife Beth. They were out!

At a bit of a loss, we caught a bus back east out of town and got off by an old stable with a smattering of civilisation and set up the tent and with some reluctance and disappointment, we consumed a tin of Dinty Moore. As dusk fell and the temperature seemed to rise to seriously warm, we wandered off to investigate this isolated oasis of Winnipeg and came across an interesting-looking bar. Our accents always seemed to draw attention and it was not long before a very beautiful looking girl and a grizzly looking old bloke had us marked down as Australians. The beautiful girl introduced us to her equally beautiful sisters and it became apparent the grizzly bloke was an uncle. He wasn't much of a chaperone as he quickly got pissed and lost interest in his charges, if in fact they were his charges. But we didn't mind, they were great company and it turned out one of the girls was Miss Manitoba 1978. I imagined the other two sisters must have come second and third as there was nothing in it. Somehow an invitation to the tent didn't seem appropriate, but she gave me her phone number!

The next morning we went back to the bar and called Sam and Beth. They were full of apologies and said, 'Stay where you are, we will drive out and collect you.' They were there in no time and stuffed us and our smelly backpacks into their small Chrysler and set off to give us an immediate tour of the town, which mainly consisted of pointing out shopping malls and Eaton's, Winnipeg's largest department store, all without stopping once. They lived in suburbia in a classical detached 1940's wood-built six-room house. They seemed fascinated by us but at the same time somewhat curious. Sam's mother had mentioned sometime earlier these two English lads may visit during the year, one of which, me, being distantly related. Equally I wasn't initially really too sure or comfortable imposing Stevie and I on complete strangers. We had decided to give it a day and see how it went before resolving if we should move on or not. Sam and Beth were mid-forties, with no children of their own. He was quite stout and muscular with dark cropped hair. He had a strong deep voice and fairly outgoing nature. She was quite twee and demure, quiet and distant with set hair and everyday sensible clothes. He was a self-employed electrician and Beth sat at home all day, which probably explained her solitary personality. Slightly out of character, she suddenly asked if we would like to have a bath as she inferred we smelt like the garbage can! Later, smelling less like a pair of red raccoons we sat and recounted some of our recent experiences and before long we all relaxed and felt lot more comfortable in each other's company. Sam said, 'I really hope you guys will stay a few days. I have to work during the day, but dinner tomorrow night is on me.'

The following day we took a local bus into town and found a park where to my great delight cricket was being played. Inevitably this included a few expats. I introduced myself as a cricket nut far from home which led to some interesting conversations with the various cricketers, particularly with one bloke who had a peculiar dislike of any England captain who lost to the Aussies, not least Mike Denness. It is incredible how an individual's prejudice travels and stays with them anywhere in the world. Suffice to say Douglas Jardine was an absolute hero. It certainly all seemed very inconsequential in Winnipeg! Canadians and Americans just don't comprehend cricket, as witnessed when a complete berk walked his dog across the outfield midway through an over. This single act confirmed my long-held belief that a foreigner is someone who doesn't understand cricket. The only trouble with this theory was that in Canada I was the foreigner!

I was amused that the captain calmly held up play until the dog walker had passed by. Do that at Priory Meadow, Hastings and you would have received a real verbal volley, wherever you were from.

We had agreed to meet Sam and Beth for dinner

at the Spaghetti Factory at 6.30p.m. Only Sam arrived, with no explanation as to why Beth wasn't there. We soon found out when Sam said, 'I'll show you guys a bit of the Winnipeg night life.' This consisted of a few seedy bars and couple of porn shops. I can't deny we had a good evening; however, the real Sam was well and truly exposed and why the straight laced Beth was left at home.

After a few quiet days watching Beth's holiday cini-films of Hawaii and playing a bit of basketball in the backyard we decided to move out before the tedium ground us down.

4.   James Bond, Calamity Jane And Close Encounters

Middle Canada stretched for hundreds of miles. It was vast and covered in prairie, mile after mile after mile of wheat as far the eye could see. It was fantastically hot, but we had to be honest with ourselves and admit it was monotonous, uninteresting and a bit boring. So rather than keep heading west through Saskatchewan on the Trans-Canada Highway, we hitchhiked due south out of town down to the border and back into the USA. We were heading for Fargo and the wonderfully named Bismark, North Dakota. We got a lift with a guy who proudly told us he had met the Queen, without explaining the 'how, when and why' bit. Anyhow he was crossing the border and would take us across, provided we did not tell the officials we were hitchhikers. We had to have a new visa stamped in our passports which seemed easy enough. When asked about our mode of transport I said 'bus'. This seemed to satisfy the immigration officer despite the obvious lack of a bus in the vicinity. Our royal friend dropped us thirty miles inside the USA.

North Dakota traffic was about as frequent as the traffic back in Wawa. After forty-five minutes, a cop driving north on the opposite carriageway spotted us and U-turned across the grass central reservation, which was like a gully. It was a wonder his car didn't get stuck down there. Anyhow he drove slowly alongside us and stopped, told us to sit in the back of his car, locked the doors, chewed his gum, said very little and drove us to Grand Forbes and wished us a good day! This was all very odd; he managed to scare the shit out of us while doing us a big favour. Like the cop outside Algonquin Park the cop car was a classic oversized American monstrosity, with red and blue lights dotted all over it, and black-and-white large chequered paintwork. There was a grill between the front and back seats, on which his rifle hung, driver side of course. I had never been in a police vehicle before, but was certain the Hastings constabulary, who tended to trundle round in old Morris Minor Travellers or Austen 1300 Panda cars at a sedate pace, would never have seen anything like this. Quite a contrast really.

We thought maybe he initially considered us to be a pair of desperadoes on the run and as soon as he heard us talk realised his mistake and acted as the Good Samaritan. His lack of communication certainly didn't help. After this we managed to secure a lift in a Dodge Broughton RV Campervan all the way to Fargo.

The one thing Stevie and I firmly agreed on was being completely flexible as our next lift may dictate where we go or could end up. Sure, we knew in which general direction to travel, but we didn't ever want to tie ourselves down to specific dates or schedule. We met a fellow hitchhiker called Lee at a place called Belfield, near the Montana state border. Lee, who had roots back east someplace, was knocking on a bit, probably early fifties. His wife had passed away and he had sold up and hit the road to see America. Classic escapism. However, Lee was a fountain of knowledge. We looked at place names on our map and decided within our agreed criteria where to go. Lee advised us well and said, 'If you are heading for Deadwood and the Blackhills of Dakota make sure you don't miss out on Mount Rushmore, it's a sight to be seen.'

Suffice to say neither of us had ever heard of Mount Rushmore, but as soon as Lee said, 'Deep Purple In Rock: the album cover', I knew we had to go there. The cover is based on the Mount Rushmore carved figure heads. I had always had a thing about album covers. There is no question the sound and the quality of the music is first and foremost (obviously), but there is something magical and tangible about an album cover. In the case of this album, the awesome 'Sweet Child in Time' anthem had converted me to rock music overnight. I felt the album cover truly reflected the material contained within the Deep Purple 'In Rock' album, but I had absolutely no idea of its origins.

But first to Deadwood. I was very vaguely aware of Doris Day and the Deadwood stagecoach, 'Whip Crack Away: Whip Crack Away' and all that stuff. I wasn't prepared for a full-blown Hollywood-style stage set of a classic cowboy ghost town, complete with the Deadwood stagecoach, Calamity Jane, cowboys, saloon bars and a tacky tourist souvenir shop disguised as the Deadwood Stores. Tannoyed music of Doris Day singing 'Whip Crack Away: Whip Crack Away' and other tasteless trash was piped down the main drag. Thirty minutes was enough of Deadwood. We high-tailed it out of there as fast as our thumbs would carry us.

By contrast we arrived in Custer State Park in the quite breathtaking Blackhills and found an official campsite for the night.

Camping and campsites in the US are very different from home. The few I had stayed on in the UK were muddy fields with basic to non-existent facilities housing a variety of canvas tents in all shapes and sizes and a few VW Dormobile campervans with those strange roof extensions, which enabled you to stand upright inside the van. Sometimes the campers would attach a canopy and prop it up with poles and broomsticks! Caravans hooked on to the back of domestic cars, half of which weren't really powerful enough to tow their dangerous cargo, which were nothing but dangerous on the narrow roads of the British Isles, as they swayed from side to side.

Here at the Custer State Park Campsite the facilities first rate, the tents generally were family size, large campervans at least twice the side of a VW Dormobile, virtually no caravans as I understood them and these giant loathsome Winnebago monstrosities. The size of an articulated lorry, they were hotels on eight wheels. They contained all the comforts of home including a fully-equipped kitchen inclusive of washing machine, shower room and beds galore, and living area with TV. It beats me why anyone would want to traipse round driving these enormous mobile condos. Surely the whole point of camping is to rough it and be as one with nature. I accept Stevie and I were taking basic camping to its lowest level out of economic necessity, but we both viewed Winnebagos and their occupants with total distain.

We got lucky again when fellow campers, Rendell and Josh from Baltimore, offered Stevie and me a lift in their car partway to Mount Rushmore.

The stone-sculpted monuments carved into the side of Mount Rushmore immortalised four US Presidents – namely Washington, Jefferson, Roosevelt and Lincoln. Tricky Dickie failed to make the cut. Originally commissioned to celebrate 150 years of US independence, the corner stone was laid by the then US President Calvin Coolidge during the summer of 1927. Coolidge may well have been a man of his time, but he was unquestionable eccentric, as he went on extraordinarily long holidays lasting up to two months at a time. In 1927 he firmly put North and South Dakota on the tourist map by spending a couple of months there dressed up as a cowboy almost every day! Not your everyday US President!

The carvings were designed and sculptured by one John Gutson Borglum and took over twelve years to complete. They are huge, awesome sculptures and quite a feat of endurance and dedication. I had no idea Deep Purple's depiction of Ian Gillan/Richie Blackmore/Roger Glover/Jon Lord had its origins here in South Dakota.

From here we hitched to the Rushmore caves, a classic cavern of stalagmites and stalactites. We had a wander around Keystone (presumably this is where the Keystones Cops originated) and hitched back to our campsite. By an amazing coincidence the first car that stopped was Rendell and Josh from Custer State Park Campsite.

'Want a lift back, guys?' Talk about a bit of luck.

We spent three nights in all at Custer Park as there was so much to see and do in the general area. On the Wednesday (28th June) we walked around the Needles. These are a unique collection of geological structures which were quite amazing. On our last night we were sleeping soundly after sharing a twelve pack with Rendell and Josh by the camp fire, when we were awoken by people yelling and shouting. A lone bovine bison had stampeded right through the campsite, clearly spooked by people and possibly the campfires. It had brushed against campervans and kicked out tent guide rope pegs as it went storming past. We were bloody lucky the beast missed us completely. Eventually, enough men in an amusing assortment of night-time attire and underwear saw it off and chased it back into the wild beyond, then went back to their slumber.

Old Lee had told us about the Badlands, and his tales of their natural beauty had been corroborated by others over the past few days. Again an area of highly unusual geological rock formations, and very rich in fossils of long extinct creatures, it had to be worth a detour. We hitched via Rapid City where a middle-aged woman stopped for us. Believe me, this was unusual for fairly obvious reasons. She had no concerns and undoubtedly welcomed some company and people to talk to. Americans generally are fascinated by our English accents. She started with the normal question 'Are you guys, Australian?' I cannot for the life of me understand why we kept being asked this. Stevie once said to a bloke in a diner 'Do we sound fucking Australian?' Of course he had no idea what an Aussie accent sounded like any more than a Scandinavian or Yugoslavian accent.

'British,' I replied politely to our lady driver.

'Well whatever you are I just *loove* your accent. You sound just like James Bond.'

Well that was a first and I assume she meant Roger Moore. I sound nothing like Roger Moore or indeed the great Scot, Sean Connery, and neither does Stevie. I was confused now; was that her best chat-up line? I guessed it wasn't as it soon became apparent she was very happily married with two small children. She was fun and full of charm and great conversation. She drove us through the Badlands on the designated loop, stopping at various viewing points. It was as stunning as we had been told. As the lady said 'Good times in the Badlands', it seemed a pretty good strapline to us.

As we had no alternative than to head for another official campsite, the nameless lady said she would drop us off at the first one we came to.

It may have been an official campsite but Sage Creek Campsite would be best described as primitive. No running water and the loo was a hole in the ground. Water was stored in large jerry cans. I was half expecting an American version of Mr Fiddler from the *Carry On Camping* movie to appear at any moment: '*Just a dollar more*'. However, it was a lovely location with grasshoppers the size of ping-pong balls! We pitched our tent next to a Welsh couple in their early forties, who were on a two-week camping holiday in a Chrysler camper touring van. John and Rhona from the Rhonda Valley were brilliant; they worked in the steel industry in Port Talbot in various capacities and were mercifully child-free, as they put it. John had a classic Welsh beer gut and like any true Welshman was rugby mad. Apart from her accent, Rhona could have come from anywhere in the British Isles. They appeared to have brought the entire contents of a supermarket with them.

We had a few cans of Millers and tin of Dinty Moore Stew and some dried bread. Once they had stopped laughing at our lack of proper food they unloaded a barbeque, slabs of red meat and chicken, fresh fish, large baking potatoes wrapped in foil, salads, and bourbon and unlimited beer. They also had a couple of large blocks of ice. They suggested we threw our tin of Dinty Moore Stew into the garbage can and join them. They didn't have to ask twice. It was an absolute pleasure to see the back of it. It actually felt like an honour to throw it into the garbage can. At 7p.m. the temperature was still hovering just below the 100 degree mark. It was the perfect night. Great company, great food and drink and we could sit back and see the Milky Way, something I had never seen before. The banter and jokes carried on well into the small hours. Sometimes you wonder if life can get any better than this. Apart from having a good woman by my side, it didn't seem likely.

We wanted to head west in the rough direction of Wyoming, John said he would run us out to the interstate 90 so we could get a head start. We were sorry to have to say goodbye to John and Rhona, but we wanted to press on and not be seen to rely on their generosity. This was going to be a classic day on the road, scrabbling from lift to lift with a varying assortment of interesting people. A couple in a station wagon, an American Indian fella in his Dodge, then a decent ride of 140 miles with a trucker hauling logs all the way to Gillette, Campbell County, Wyoming.

Climbing into a Kenworth Cab was actually quite humbling. US truckers are iconic with their hulking wagons, powerful engines under a vast protruding bonnet, twin vertical exhaust pipes and enormous square front grills. The cabs are not only the driving hub, it's also where a lot of the guys eat and sleep. Some are huge and look like a front room, fully inclusive with portable TV! Ninety-five percent of the trucks look straight out of the workshop, gleaming paintwork and sparkling chrome and their vertical twin exhausts reaching up the side of the cab skywards.

Compared with home, where old flatbed trucks and curtain-sided lorries chug along belching acrid smoke and look a little sorry for themselves, over here they have great pride and passion in their vehicles and even hold 'truck conventions'. The advent of the CB Radio had built up a whole trucking culture, to the point where an amusing record was released a couple of years ago, 'Convey' by C W McCoy, which was a hit both sides of the Atlantic. 10/4!

Gillette would have been real frontier country back in the day. Now it was bit depressing, quite industrial, a real working town. None of the past remained, it been flattened to accommodate post-war industry. We pitched our tent by a timber yard and bought ourselves a huge pizza – my new favourite food.

The next morning we did some very rare washing at a local launderette and headed out to the freeway. After five minutes a cop pulled up and informed us hitchhiking was illegal in Wyoming, issued us an informal warning and drove off. As he disappeared over the horizon we hitched a lift! And what a lift: 414 miles over eight hours all the way to somewhere called Jackson Hole with an anonymous car and driver. The radio was tuned into the country music channel and blared out non-stop country. To me, one country record sounds very much like the next. I can tell you after eight hours I never want to hear another bloody country record ever again; it was purgatory! However, this one lift vindicated our decision not to plan where we went.

Jackson Hole lies in the foothills of the Grand Teton Mountain range, is a tourist spot, maybe more popular in the winter when the ski slopes are in action. It looked interesting and quite different to the average run-of-the-mill American town we had seen so far. It was getting dark when we arrived so we pitched the tent in some long grass just outside of town, then strolled in to take a look about. We found a bar, had a few beers and a burger and decided to head back to the tent. The only trouble was it was now pitch black. The good people of Jackson Hole had gone to bed and turned all the lights out. Fortunately we did have a torch, but it was as good as useless as the batteries were running down. We stumbled around for a good couple of hours in the total darkness, crashing into low hedgerows and barbed wire; we somehow walked into a field of cattle and horses. Stevie almost inevitably stood in a large pile of steaming horse manure, much to his disgust and my delight. Eventually by sheer good chance we came across our isolated tent. Stevie left his boots outside, no one was going to nick these!

The one thing that did become clear as we were once again in a National Park was that we would have to find an official campsite and stump up the cash, so first thing in the morning we returned to a now-vibrant Jackson Hole to stock up on supplies including the revolting Dinty Moore Stew, as much as we hated it, but at just over a dollar a tin it was best value, plus fruit, veg, bread and cheese, then we set out to hitch to the Grand Teton National Park. We made it there with a couple of lifts by late morning, only to find every campsite full for the July 4th celebrations just a couple of days ahead. We got talking to a Norwegian couple and they agreed to share their pitch for half the money if we were prepared to stay for the next three nights as they were. That suited us all just fine. We spent the afternoon doing a six-mile hike around picture-postcard-perfect Jenny Lake. The royal blue water of the lake was hemmed in on one side by monstrous mountains and all the rest of the rim by sloping green hills covered with pine trees. I guess it was very Swiss in appearance but not having been to Switzerland it was hard to say.

Back at the campsite I heard an English accent. It was a fellow traveller on the road from Surrey, one Geoffrey McStuart-Racionnzer who was obsessed with travelling the world, Chelsea FC and Wasps RFU. We shared a couple of six packs with him. It was actually quite refreshing to talk football and rugby once more instead of baseball and American football, which I was still struggling to get my head round, along with Geoffrey's name.

You can't tell the Yanks this, but professional American football seems a pointless and futile sport. Clearly manufactured for television advertising, it takes four hours to complete a one hour game of rough and tumble in body armour. Very strange.

Geoffrey was keen to keep the repartee going the next day, so the three of us set off on a long gruelling ten-mile hike to Solitude Lake via the oddly named Paintbrush Canyon. It was a seriously steep climb, about 3000 feet. At about the halfway point we hit the ice line. It was way into the high eighties and yet underfoot was compacted ice to a depth of over forty foot. We were shirtless walking on ice. On the way back I slipped down a slope and slid about twenty yards, but managed to cling on to the one solitary tree. If I had missed this it would have been a further two-hundred yards on my arse, down a steep icy bank. The gods again were smiling on me. I'm a lucky fool.

We were pretty fit, but the next morning, the 4th July, I was aching all over and my feet wanted a day off. Stevie and Geoffrey had hitched into Jackson to buy supplies but I decided to stay local to the campsite and got lucky.

She was a Kansas girl out for a good time. She told me her friends called her Amber. Amber was no beauty, an ordinary body with a few nice curves. Her hair was auburn red, her face plain, but she had a naughty smile like a Wicked Angel. My non-existent James Bond accent worked its charm and she took me to her canvas boudoir. Fortunately her friends had also gone to Jackson for a few hours too. She certainly wasn't backward at coming forward and I wasn't going to say no. She saw no irony at being screwed by a Brit on American Independence day. Maybe she thought I was Australian?

The next day Amber was heading home to Wichita and Stevie and I decided to head for Yellowstone. We got stuck in Nowhereville, Idaho for over three hours, when a guy in a very classy campervan with his two young sons aged eight and ten pulled over for us. Maurice was, as he put it, a Wyoming cowboy made good. He was also the best guy we had met to date. He was on exactly our wavelength, got our obscure British humour and was brilliant at taking the piss out of life in general. He was hysterically funny and also one of the most outgoing and generous of individuals anyone could hope to meet. He was relatively local, living and operating his various businesses out of Jackson Hole. He had taken his lads for a spin in the campervan but clearly found it hard to contain his wild side even with his boys in tow.

'Let's stop for a beer,' he said. And did! This had to be normal behaviour as far as the young lads were concerned as they were straight at the bar and demanded a soda and chips.

'Look where you guys heading and what you doing tonight?' asked Maurice. Stevie explained our mantra, our way of life on the road, avoiding campsites whenever possible and our ambitious budget of $3 dollars per day expenditure.

'Oh God, fuck that,' said Maurice. 'You can't enjoy yourself with such limitations. You guys come and stay with us tonight and we can all go hunting beaver.'

I didn't know what the heck he was talking about, until the ten-year-old told me that was American slang for women. Thank God for little boys! This kid was mature beyond his years.

'Well thanks, Maurice, great offer, but we don't want to go back to Jackson. We have just come from there and it would be going in the wrong direction for us,' I said.

'Not Jackson. Here in Yellowstone. I'll book you into our motel, have dinner and hit the bars.'

'Look we can't afford that.'

'Aw shucks, I am not asking you to pay, I'll cover the cheque.'

Maurice was insistent and true to his word. He booked us a twin room, paid for a stack of ribs and fries. At 9.30 he took his kids upstairs, they took the whole bizarre episode in their stride. He came back to the bar and bought double Irish whiskeys all round. Unfortunately or possibly fortunately, there didn't seem to be much available beaver or women about. As the whiskeys went down we got talking to a guy from Hollywood, who had the unusual name of Barry Barrie. He told us he was a 'location manager' and was scouting Yellowstone for potential sites for a movie version of *Star Trek*. This fella was keeping pace with the doubles and was happy to keep going all night, he wanted to outdrink us. He told Maurice he was always on the lookout for beaver as well. I guess most men are, but we thought he was a bit creepy and were secretly glad we didn't get to see him chatting up a bird.

'So you guys like your whiskey do ya?' he asked.

I looked him in the eye, 'Sure thing.'

'We all love our booze,' added Maurice.

'That could be interesting,' replied Barry Barrie.

We left him under the table at two in the morning and staggered upstairs.

I didn't know where we were, somewhere on the edge of the Yellowstone National Park. We could have been in Idaho, Wyoming or Montana! I wasn't even sure what day it was. One thing I knew for sure was my head hurt liked hell. At 10a.m., over coffee, Maurice said 'Right let's all go see the geysers and hot springs.' We had a great morning seeing all the main attractions. I could see why the *Star Trek* guy was here, these thermal geysers were far out and did look like they belonged in a different world.

Sitting in Maurice's campervan he suddenly became quite serious:

'Guys I have a business proposition for you. You come back to Jackson and work for me in my souvenir gift shops, I have two. Virtually all the tourists are either American or Canadian and your British accents and personalities will go down a storm with them. I'll pay you $150 dollars a week each with free lodgings over the one of the shops. However, it would have to be for a minimum of three months to the end of the summer season. What do ya'll think?'

This was an incredibly tempting offer and would revolutionise our dwindling finances. It would be cash in hand and no questions asked. But three months was more than we could agree to. It would be October before we left Jackson, it would just muck up our timescales (back to New York) and we would have to compromise our travelling too much.

Stevie and I had a long chat about it. We were both really torn as Maurice was a top bloke and knew we would have enjoyed the experience, but ultimately decided against Maurice's truly magnanimous offer. We did say to him we would be happy to give it a couple of weeks, but he insisted three months or no deal. So it was with genuine sorrow and some regret we said goodbye to Maurice. He was understandably disappointed, but wished us well and we agreed to go our separate ways.

Stevie's 1977 trip to North America had included the Canadian Rockies, which he said were great and I would 'love it for sure'. He wanted to revisit a few places and maybe look up a couple of people he had met with last time round. So we decided to head north again through Wyoming and Montana, heading for the Canadian border on the Alberta demarcation line. Leaving Yellowstone about 3p.m., with my head feeling no better, we did get a couple of quick lifts. At some point we were dropped in a very small town with one main central road, we drank some coffee and asked the waitress which way to the highway. She was maybe thirty-five, slim and looked reasonably fit and stepped outside the door with us to point north-east.

'It's a good mile, straight up there,' she said. 'I can call you a taxi to take you.'

'No that will be alright, we will walk,' said Stevie.

'But it's over a mile,' she insisted.

'No problem, we can easily walk that,' Steve smiled.

She looked dumbfounded, 'I could never walk that far. Not sure many people could.'

Not wishing to patronise her, I said, 'We've had a bit of experience at walking long distances,' and marched off.

The mid-west is beautiful, rugged, barren and vast. We were with a guy in a small delivery lorry and he said, 'Did you see the Steve Spielberg movie last year *Close Encounters of the Third Kind*? Did you get that in the UK?'

The answer from both of us was yes it was and yes we did.

'OK,' says our driver, 'do you recognise that?' nodding to his right. And there it was, the tall mound which featured in the film, which Richard Dreyfuss obsessed about. It was really eerie seeing this huge, tall cylindrical granite mound with a flat top standing alone in the wilderness.

'Well its real name is the "Devil's Tower" and it's the very first US National Monument opened by Roosevelt in 1906. It's a real landmark hereabouts. It has thousands of visitors from all over the country who come here for the peace and tranquillity and also many rock climbers – it's no easy climb – I should know, I have tried and failed.'

Sadly we sailed on right past it and kept driving over the state line into Montana.

Again we had no real idea where we were other than we were in 'Big Sky Country', as Montana is known, and pitched our tent in a field near to the side of the road. The sun was setting low in the monstrous sweeping sky. We were completely knackered and had a great night's kip, waking at about nine o'clock the next morning feeling alive once more.

5. Big Joel, Synthetic Sausage And The Shit Shoveler

Talk about a stroke of luck, after just five minutes thumbing, a van with four Oxbridge students pulled in for us. They were en route to Calgary, the largest city in Alberta and now so were we!

Our philosophy of 'blow with the wind' was paying off. God knows what they made of Stevie and me; we were intellectually light years apart from these post-graduates. These chaps had degrees in the modern greats or PPE (Philosophy, Politics and Economics). We had a few low-level grades in A-level Economic History and Business Studies. Plus I had a 'B' in European and American Modern History 1776-1918. They were all former public-school boys and we went to the abysmal Grove! Stevie said to me later he thought that one or two of them were probably future cabinet ministers! However, a combination of music and sport found a common denominator. They were also touring around the locality, staying in nice hotels, eating at decent restaurants, like, it has to be said, most other tourists. Ultimately their holiday would culminate in a trip to the Commonwealth Games to be staged in Edmonton sometime in August. In some ways they were beguiled by our 'hitchhike around North America, have no money, couldn't give a damn' attitude, which could not have been far more removed from theirs.

We spent a night on the edge of town. From what I

could see, Calgary didn't look particularly interesting. I knew nothing about Calgary, other than the city hosts a large rodeo event each year known as the 'Stampede'. It didn't really hold much interest for us – and was possibly over for this year anyhow – so we decided to press on the next day to Edmonton where Stevie knew a fella called Andy he had met the year before, who had driven him all the way from Salt Lake City.

Andy, Stevie said, lived in a suburb called Strathcona in a very large house of wood construction possibly built around the time of the First World War. The exterior was painted in pastel shades of blue, pink and yellow.

Whoever the fella, Andy, from the year before, was not in when we knocked unannounced on his front door. However, his housemates Kim and Elaine were in.

'Andy is on holiday in Montreal, but if you are friends of Andy's and you want a stay a few nights it's not a problem – come in and make yourself at home!' North American hospitality was quite amazing. We were complete strangers, but they had no compunction about welcoming us into their home. I guess we should have been hugely embarrassed and said something like 'no we couldn't possibly'. But actually we said 'thanks very much' and walked in. Stevie looked blank and confirmed, 'These people weren't here last year. But what the heck'!

Kim was a real music fan and I was delighted to find a copy of John Mayall's 'Turning Point' in his collection.

Stevie definitely liked Edmonton and was keen to stay a few nights. I wasn't quite so sure. I was actually embarrassed at imposing ourselves on Kim and Elaine; however the next day we were exploring Edmonton when we came across an expansive park and to my amazement there was a proper game of cricket being played on a properly prepared wicket. Inevitably we got talking to some of the guys and were introduced to the first team captain Douglas Mathias. An interesting bloke, half Geordie, half South African; quite a combination it has to be said. He asked if we played and I said, 'Yes, but not to your standard.' He offered me an opportunity to play an evening match for his second XI which I jumped at. Stevie said he was no good at cricket and would sit it out. Mr Mathias was a fountain of cricketing knowledge, statistics and facts. He said, 'Did you know the very first international cricket match ever played was between the USA and Canada, staged in Manhattan in 1844?'

'No, I can't say I was aware of that,' I replied.

'Furthermore that match was the very first sporting international game of any sport, anywhere.' That truly was an astounding and interesting part of sporting history. Mr Mathias than rattled on a bit about more North American bits of useless historical cricket facts such as the only first-class cricketer to go down on the *Titanic* was one John Borland Thayer Jr, formally of Philadelphia CC. It had to be true, because you just couldn't make that up. However, I digress...

I flattered myself that I could bat at six. This giant big

West Indian fella who looked like Joel Garner steamed in – all six foot eight of him. A red blur pitched well up around off stump gave me an opportunity to put bat on ball. Except I was too late; red blur smashes in to off stump first ball. Innings over, my technique exposed, my ego and enthusiasm took a huge hit, as I marched back to the Pavilion to a sea of disappointed faces. I was beginning to believe this bloke was Joel Garner, but then again what was Joel Garner doing in Canada and what was he doing playing the second XI club cricket? These guys were way out of my league.

Normally during the interval between innings at home the wives and girlfriends produce a sumptuous tea of assorted sandwiches, pork pies, cakes, tea and fruit juices. I was flabbergasted not to mention miffed, when I was offered a hamburger and a bottle of root beer. I guess not everything about the British cricket heritage made it across the Atlantic.

During the second innings I was kindly given a bowl and felt I had some real revolutions on the ball as it left my hand. By the time the ball had reached the other end, the revolutions had dissipated and the ball sailed out of the ground. I wasn't invited back! Returning to Kim and Elaine, I started to explain my cricket experience but realised very soon I had completely lost their interest. Cricket and Canadians just weren't meant to be, I guess.

We spent a further five nights with our hosts, who we really got to like. If they had been ten years older I would have considered them as aged hippies from the sixties, but they were only a couple of years older than us. They liked a few beers and Elaine especially liked a few joints. I confessed to her I had hardly ever touched marijuana. She said 'you haven't lived unless you smoke a few joints' and insisted I joined her. It was a crazy experience, it felt like I was in a dream while very much awake. Every sense was enhanced, the Hendrix Electric Ladyland album on Kim's quite excellent stereo system sounded better than ever. Everything felt a little weird and I suddenly had a craving for crisps. It was so strong I felt I just had to go out and buy a bag somewhere. I ran down the road in the vain hope of coming across a store. After trying three or four more blocks, I found a corner store and asked for crisps. The man behind the counter didn't know what I was talking about. I kept saying 'you must sell crisps' and was getting quite agitated when he suddenly produced a bag, which he said were called chips. My understanding was chips came wrapped in newspaper from the local fish & chip shop; however, chips in Canada are called French fries, all very confusing, especially when you are as high as a kite. My appetite and craving sated, I ran back to the house for another joint.

Friday 14th July we upped and left our bohemian friends after a lunch of marmite sandwiches and chips – or was that crisps? The Rockies had long been an imperative on our 'must visit' list. Again Stevie repeated the unique beauty of the Rockies and said it was the best time he had last year, before the 'Reverend' Marcus Ball had thrown the towel in and buggered off home. Jasper was the starting point. We got a lift in a chartreuse microbus with three friends of Jesus (honestly, it's true) virtually all the way. It took a while to make the last twenty miles; we found a bar for refreshments and pitched the tent in a field at the back of Jasper infants' school.

We took the tent down first thing that morning and decamped to a coffee bar for an hour or so. After stocking up our meagre rations at the local 7-Eleven store we walked a couple of miles in the pouring rain to the Whistlers Camp Ground in Jasper National Park, which had been recommended to us last evening. By midday we were set up and Stevie asked a couple of guys from Wisconsin if he could borrow their axe to chop a bit of firewood. The last thing they said was 'sure, but don't break it.' Sure enough Stevie managed to snap the willow shaft in two. I'd never seen him go so red or so animated.

'Oh fuck, fuck, fuck, fuck, how am I going to explain this? What do I say?'

'Sorry?' I suggested.

Steve glared at me. He was seriously wound up. As he still had the axe in his hand I backed off and left him to account for his misfortune to the irked campers next door and hid a good distance back to stifle my uncontrollable laughter at both his and their misfortune.

During the evening at the camp 'leisure area' we met an English bloke from Gravesend called Dave Kiln. He was on his own and had a fixation about climbing mountains. He was small, supple, wiry and as tough as an ox. Fortunately he also had a classic British sense of humour and from the first moment we really hit it off. The three of us sat around the campfire talking and drinking all night with the two vexed axe men from Wisconsin, until the rumble of thunder and bolts of lightning drove us to our tents.

In the morning the campground was awash, streams of water everywhere and campers wringing out soaked clothing and bedding. A smug camper emerging from his campervan quickly came down to earth when his foot sunk into a very wet muddy patch and went arse overhead, covering him in mud, sludge and shit. He didn't look best pleased as he stormed off to the wash rooms. Indeed for me and Steve taking advantage of good toiletry facilities was important, given how many nights we spent in fields and roadsides where no plumbing whatsoever was available. An obvious advantage of a properly maintained campsite, however poor the drainage, was the ability to take full advantage to complete the daily ablutions or the 'Five S's. This stood for Shit: Shower: Scrub: Shave and Shampoo. On the road I hated shaving in cold water and crapping in the bushes. So having duly completed these requirements in some sort of comfort, we joined Dave on a hike to Maligne Canyon. It was a good eight miles' hike. The canyon was about 100 feet deep but only 6 feet wide. Dave was climbing up and down it like a demented monkey. His strength, fitness and energy were astonishing. He seemed to be able to sprint up and down vertical slopes at speed without losing balance or looking in any trouble whatsoever. We then hiked back to the campsite only for Dave to shin up a tree to retrieve his rucksack containing his food. It wasn't so much he could shin up a tree it was more that he did at such phenomenal speed and apparent lack of effort. Stevie wondered if he was bionic. Dave's caution, however, was fully justified, as an hour later a black bear came strolling into the campsite sniffing out the campers' dinners and other goodies. Not even a black bear could reach our food dangling thirty foot in the air. The last thing anyone wants to do is tangle with these mighty creatures, but a cacophony of noise by banging pots and pans normally scares the grizzlies off.

We spent a couple of quieter days in and around Jasper. Although we had to pay a bit over the odds, which completely blew our $3 a day budget for these in-demand National Park campsites, they were without question great social centres. The obvious common denominator was for everyone camping and exploring the Rockies, which just have to be among the most beautiful places in the world, but also the comradeship and togetherness it built between strangers from all over North America and the rest of the world was extraordinary. There were very few loners at the campsites. As such it was good fun talking to people from such diverse places as Brazil, New Zealand, South Africa, right across the European continent and of course the relative locals from the US and Canada. The only downside for Stevie and I and possibly a few others like Dave Kiln was our budgets didn't let us stretch to decent food. We ate some disgusting campfire meals such as synthetic sausage and tinned spaghetti. Another time we bought a tin of beans with 'pork'; the pork was one lump of fat which melted when heated. It was so bad we had to chuck it away and ate stale bread. Of course Dinty Moore Stew was a staple; it may taste like crap, but at least we could just about eat it!

A lot of the North Americans enjoyed roasting marshmallows over the barbeque. I don't get it. Marshmallows may or may not be better than Dinty More Stew, but what is so special about marshmallows? I mean what's it all about? It strikes me as such a weird American cultural tradition.

Dave was great company and kept us entertained throughout. He invented a game of 'spot the Englishman abroad'. This all started when we spotted a chap in his fifties with fair hair, trimmed moustache, a beak of a nose, National Health glasses, and a forehead as high as the Rockies, wearing polished brown sandals with dark woollen socks, baggy khaki shorts, a country check shirt and white floppy sunhat. This bloke could not have looked more like an eccentric Englishman abroad if he had tried.

'I'd bet my house on it that bloke's a Brit,' uttered Dave. It was obvious he was.

'OK, go and ask him then,' said Steve. Dave duly did and came back with a grin and said, 'His name is Clemence Leggit and he's from Wiltshire.' We weren't bold enough to ask every potential Brit where they were from, but we were more right than we were wrong most of the time. Sandals with socks are a dead giveaway!

The flip side of Dave was he could be a bit direct at times, especially towards anyone who didn't really pick up or understand his humour. Twice he managed to unintentionally offend fellow Brits. There was a guy from Northallerton in Yorkshire who said he worked on his dad's farm, 'Flint Rock Farm,' he said proudly. Dave called him a 'shit shoveler'. He didn't look too pleased and ignored us for the rest of the night. Then there was a plain teenage white girl camping with her parents. She proudly told us she was from Birmingham, 'Oh yeah,' said Dave, 'where's your turban?' I didn't think it was that offensive, it was just a weak attempt at humour, but she burst into tears. However, I did think it a bit rich coming from a bloke from Gravesend. Dave shrugged his shoulders and left her sobbing. I guess if people didn't get him, he didn't care.

By Wednesday it was time to move on to the next well-documented Rockies tourist hot spot, to a place called Lake Louise in Banff National Park. A difficult day on the road culminated in a park warden giving us a lift partway along the Colombia Icefields Highway. It was great to have a personal guide, the scenery was quite outstanding. The last fifty miles Stevie and I bounced around in the back of a dirty pickup truck but at least it got us to Lake Louise.

The following day we left all our gear in the Park Rangers' Mountain Office and had a very enjoyable hike around the lake. The lake itself is set in a glacial mountain, five and half thousand feet above sea level. I was fascinated to walk under a couple of huge, long, ice arches and take in some quite exquisite views across the lake and the mountains. We collected our gear and hitched our way to our next official campsite called Tunnel Mountain Campground outside of Banff to meet up again with Dave Kiln. For once we had prearranged this rendezvous. To our surprise the Northallerton farmer was also there. I think Dave made a bit of a half-hearted apology or maybe I apologised for Dave but from that point we all became good friends with a common cause. The farmer's name was also Dave, so to save confusion he was quickly renamed 'Mr Yorkshire', which he seemed to like and the four of us had a great night around the campfire on a diet of beer and bourbon.

Dave had talked Stevie and me into walking/climbing up to the top of Sulphur Mountain on Saturday. We invited Mr Yorkshire to join us for the experience. It was good couple of miles' walk to Banff then a further two and half miles uphill just to reach the base of the mountain. Then the hard work really started, all 2300 feet of it, but we did it and felt good about it. There weren't many people negotiating the loose stone and slate scree slopes; most whom were like David, keen mountain-climbers with all the right gear and fitness to match. There are varying degrees of fitness and most of these guys were mega-fit. In fact, very few First Diversion footballers could have been much fitter. Steve and I were very Fourth Division by comparison.

We scrambled around the top of Sulphur Mountain, breathing it all in. I had no idea if I would ever come here again and I wanted to really savour the moment. The air at the top was undoubtedly thinner, but the view was spectacular in the extreme. The effort was well rewarded. Dave pointed out a lot of the American tourists were coming from the cable cars and straight into the tearoom, barely glancing at the exotic scenery surrounding them. We felt we had deserved a cup of tea for our efforts and joined the self-service queue. Tea Canadian-style is not to be recommended; hot water in a glass, Liptons teabags placed on a saucer and help yourself to as many plastic tubs of UHT milk as you want. This caused Dave to have another of his direct 'cutting remark' moments, when he asked the poor serving girl 'for proper milk in a jug, not this chemical stuff in a plastic tub'.

'Proper milk, sir?' she questioned.

'Yea, real milk.'

'This is milk, sir,' she came back.

'No it's not, I want the white stuff that comes out of a cow,' snorted Dave.

'This is milk, sir,' she repeated.

Dave was getting visibly annoyed. 'This isn't bloody milk. It says UHT and is full of 'E' numbers and synthetic shit; it has been nowhere near a cow's udder.' It was becoming Pythonesque. He started to read out loud the 'E' numbers.

To the serving girl's credit she held her ground and said, 'Sir, that is all we have. If you can find a cow up here you can get your own Goddamn milk!'

That caused a round of applause from some onlookers and howls of laughter all round. The serving girl wasn't as timid or as weak as she looked. Dave for once lost his sense of humour; he clearly didn't like to be beaten at his own game. Mr Yorkshire, rejoicing in Dave's discomfort, slapped him on the thigh and said, 'Aye up, she fucked you over there good and proper. If thou can dish it out you have to take it back!' Clearly Mr Yorkshire got real satisfaction from Dave's humiliation. I think we all did.

The good news was there was no charge to come down the mountain in the cable car and we all got lucky when a camper from the Tunnel Mountain Campsite said we could all climb into the back of his pickup truck and took us all the way back.

The following day with the mercury really ramping up we went to visit a place called Johnson Lake a few miles from us. It was quite beautiful there. Returning to the tent about 2p.m. we decided to sunbathe for a few hours as it was so hot. A couple of well-heeled and brash Canadian guys had pitched up opposite us. I didn't get their names. They drove a sporty Fiat X19 soft top. To be fair to them they were going out of their way to be friendly towards us and said, "If one of you blokes wants to come with us in to Banff you can. We just wanna go and buy some beers and smokes.' Stevie said he would go and also fetch some more beers for us. He squeezed in on a ledge which substituted a back seat and off they went.

Forty-five minutes they were back with Stevie in the driver's seat. They had asked him if he wanted to give the X19 a spin and Stevie said he had opened it up and nearly ran a Winnebago off the road! He said, 'Worse than that, I asked if it was a dual carriageway and they said yes, so I went level with the Winnebago only to see a couple of cars coming straight towards me, so I floored the pedal and just squeezed past. The Winnebago driver was flashing his lights and blowing his horn and nearly shit himself.' This explained why the Canadian guys looked a bit white.

'So why'd you say it's a dual carriageways if it isn't?' I enquired of the car owners.

'Lost in translation, I guess,' said the whitest.

Stevie opened a couple of beers and handed them to the guys.

'Look, sorry I guess but it was a genuine misinterpretation.'

They were ready for another campfire party to celebrate still being alive and Mr Yorkshire and Dave Kiln joined in the fun.

Monday 24th was going to be our last full day at Banff. We'd had a wonderful week or so together and the four of us agreed to push the boat out and go into town. We found a half-decent diner by Bow Falls and treated ourselves to steak and chips and ice cream during the afternoon. It was a good way to say goodbye. We exchanged home addresses and promised to keep in touch.

During the night at some ungodly hour I became aware of someone or something moving around the outside of the tent. I unzipped the tent opening only to see a bear sniffing around our abandoned campfire. It clearly had the scent of something and was mooching about knocking into trees, cars, campervans and most worryingly of all sniffing at the tents. Shit, I thought, if this bear decides to rip open a tent it will be really dangerous for someone and I didn't want that someone to be me or my mates or anyone else for that matter. I said to Stevie, 'Should we bang our pots and pans?' and he said, 'Not sure – if the bear feels trapped, he could turn on us.' Fortunately by this time a few campers were aware of the imminent danger and people started to shout and make general noises. Before long, a campground warden appeared with a rifle held across his chest and started barking instructions to everyone to stay calm. The rifle was loaded with tranquilizer darts. Fortunately the bear sauntered off back into the trees without a care in the world and the excitement for the night was over. I was pleased; I really didn't want to see this big hairy mammal shot, if only with a tranquilizer. You can't blame the bears, after all this is their domain. Human activity and waste are bound to attract them and evidenced by the fact the warden had his gun at the ready this was an all too frequent occurrence.

We had an address of another obscure but distant relation on my father's side, (albeit supplied to me by Sam and Beth back in Winnipeg) at a place called Kimberley. Everywhere in British Colombia is beautiful, especially the Rockies general region, and Kimberley was no exception. Another alpine resort which possibly saw more activity in the winter than summer, it had wonderful vistas and lakes. Bizarrely it also had a strong Bavarian feel about the 'downtown' area where Bill, Viv and Linda lived. I don't know, but presumably the area was originally settled by Germans or Austrians or suchlike. However, Bavarian or not it had the classical North American tacky makeover. I made the mistake of telling Linda, 'This is all too American.'

'Canadian,' she corrected me, I ploughed on and held my ground. 'Well same thing really.'

Canadians are rightly proud of being Canadians, but to us Brits the only way to tell them apart is to offend a Canadian by calling them American, who will put you right pretty damn quick. Linda came back quite sharpish, 'Canada is Canada and the States is the States; we are two separate countries.'

They may believe they have separate national identities but culturally and socially they are identical, the people all sound the same, accept Canadians say 'Eh' all the time. The only thing that differentiates the two is an invisible line called the border.

6. Okanagan Iron Jaw, Beer And Peaches

Stevie and I were concerned at our shrinking finances. The campsite fees and general expenses were really eating into our cash and we needed to find some work to put us back on track. Bill said not so far from Kimberley was a place named Osoyoos, which was famed for its fruit orchards. He felt if we went down there we might be able to find a casual job fruit picking. We were of course on a tourist visa and officially any sort of work was completely off limits. We would need to produce a Canadian 'Permanent Resident's Card' the equivalent of the American 'Green Card' to work legally. However casual work could be possible if we hunted around.

We stayed in Kimberley a couple of days before heading off for Osoyoos.

We were now out of the Rockies and on lower ground in a valley known as the Okanagan Valley. The temperature was incredible, nearing the 100F mark. It was late afternoon and still sixty miles short of Osoyoos, but it was just too hot to do anything, so we found a field by a river and sunbathed for a few hours. At dusk we found an old abandoned log barn, which was a perfect place to spend the night – peaceful, quiet, and miles from anywhere.

Waking early Saturday morning feeling refreshed and a little hungry we hit the road by 8a.m. and got a lift right away straight into Osoyoos. We bought ourselves a decent breakfast and asked about fruit farms vis-à-vis fruit picking jobs. The local folks were quite helpful and gave us a few addresses and directions. It took a while but Stevie hit lucky and said he had found a peach orchard and they would take us on at C$3.75 per hour if we were prepared to give them two weeks' labour. It seemed the orchard would take as many people who came forward and didn't ask any questions regarding work permits etc. Start 6a.m. on Monday and we could stay at a cabin on site for free, but it was down to us to supply our own food and drink. It wasn't negotiable and we weren't going to turn it down. In fact we both thought it was a good deal, given our limited choice and dwindling cash reserves. The sun's thermostat was on maximum again today so we found a secluded part on the Osoyoos Lake and spent a very lazy day lying out in the sun and swimming in the lake. The Sunday was much the same. Having spent a bit of cash buying food provisions we made our way out to the peach orchard at 5p.m. as arranged. We introduced ourselves and we were told we would be bunking down in cabin seven. Cabin seven was just a very basic log cabin with three tatty wafer-thin mattresses, a grimy looking sink and basic shower, an antiquated stove contraption and fridge which may or may not have worked and not much else. The third bed was occupied by a Swiss fella by the name of Noah. We hadn't managed to buy any beer earlier because Canada was experiencing one of its all-too-frequent brewery strikes. The three key producers in Canada are Carling, Labetts and Molson. It was just impossible to buy a bottle or can of anything.

As the orchard farm was situated just one mile from the US border, Noah suggested we could go across in his clapped-out pickup truck to buy some beer and return in no time at all. There was a small town just south of the border called Oroville we could head for. It sounded straight forward but we had a Canadian visa which had three months to run and would have to acquire a US visa then hope we could get a new Canadian three-month visa on the way back. Well we needed beer so we went for it, just hop over the BC border into Washington State, buy twenty-four cans of beer each and return. Easy!

The border guards and custom officers were semi-sympathetic and cooperative to our desire for beer and stamped our passports in both directions with the necessary authorisation.

We were woken the following morning at 5.20 ready to start work at 6a.m. We were driven by a farm truck to the work area. The foreman was a tough-looking, no-nonsense character called Darrell with an angular jaw, denims and a grubby cream Stetson. He was straight out of central casting. Darrell put us in teams of three – naturally Stevie, me and Noah made a team. We were given a very large back basket each and a couple of ten-foot-tall wooden ladders which formed an apex at the top like a giant drawing compass. We were allocated a 'sector' and told to strip all the trees of every single peach. Once the baskets were full we were to empty them into large bunkers placed at strategic points around the orchard.

'Now get to it,' barked Darrell. 'I won't tolerate

any slackers. Anyone not giving his all will be out of here.'

'Not sure I am going to like this bastard,' said I. 'I hope he doesn't turn out to be a sadistic shite.' Stevie coined the name 'Iron Jaw', which seemed a great description of his persona and physical features.

I guessed there were in the region of a hundred peach pickers on the site. We certainly weren't the only Europeans. I heard an interesting range of languages – Italian, Spanish, Portuguese and Dutch. Not so many Mexicans or South Americans (probably one border too many for most of them) and an assortment of Yanks and Canadians. The orchard spread over a good many hectares of lush fertile land. It had to be a good three miles square. There were hundreds of peaches on every tree, ranging from small-apple-size peaches to large grapefruit size. The largest and the ripest were inevitably at the top, so we clambered up the ladders grabbing at every fruit we could reach. And we had to reach them; 'Iron Jaw' accepted no excuses and berated anyone, with some real choice language, for not clearing fruit left on the branches.

By midday, after just one fifteen-minute rest break, we were all sweating like pigs and tiring. No matter how much water we drank we were all feeling dehydrated. It was a hundred in the shade and there wasn't much of that, especially at the top of a twelve-foot peach tree. We stopped for a thirty-minute lunch break and crashed out in the shade and ate sandwiches and corn cobs. The day finished at 3p.m. The last few hours took forever to complete; this was seriously hard work. Feeling absolutely knackered we all went for a swim in the lake, showered and ate a large dinner washed down with a few Michelob beers. The next four days were all exactly the same. We fell out of bed, splashed some water, climbed on to the back of the truck and climbed up a peach tree. Noah quit after our first four days, he had already been there for a couple of weeks. A Scottish guy replaced him both in our cabin and in our team. 'You can call me AK,' he said, I never did discover his real name. He said he came from some unpronounceable Scottish Glen, but I got the impression he was an itinerant fruit picker, travelling wherever the work took him over the last couple of years, floating around Canada and the States. AK was certainly quiet and secretive. He owned a twenty-year-old brown Chevy. I think it was it was brown; there was so much rust it was hard to tell. Stevie was convinced he was either on the run or hiding from something or someone. We felt it best not to ask.

On the Friday, Darrell the Iron Jaw said to us 'You two guys can take tomorrow off.' I wasn't expecting that, but equally, despite a day without pay, welcomed an opportunity to recharge the batteries. I had never known five such intense days. The heat was like something I had never experienced before, let alone worked in. Just this week alone Stevie and I both believed we had lost three or four pounds in weight via a combination of physical activity and sweat. On the plus side we weren't spending a dime and were making thirty Canadian dollars each per day so between us we were already C$300 ahead. That did make it feel worthwhile.

We had decided to have a lazy day by the lake shore, swimming and chilling out. We met a French girl by the name of Francine who was quite stunning. She was also peach picking and staying in a cabin. It is very difficult to chat up a bird when your mate is by your side and won't take the hint to sod off. The reason was easy to understand as Stevie was equally infatuated with Francine. I guess we were in competition with each other as to which one of us could pull her first! The problem was resolved when a French-Canadian guy started chatting her up in her native tongue and before we knew it they were up and gone. I had to admit to being bloody furious with the Canadian guy, with Francine and with Stevie. I was being too bloody British and polite and had her snatched away by someone who was clearly a lot more direct: it was fairly obvious from the way she behaved she was equally gagging for it. I bought a beer and brooded all evening, while the Commodores' 'Three Times a Lady' played in the background. Probably not the most appropriate record under the circumstances. I hadn't felt this pissed off since I worked in the pickle factory in Hastings! It seemed like an early night and a wank was all I had left to look forward to. But even that was off the cards when we got back to the cabin to find the sink blocked and the room engulfed in an overwhelming stench in the unrelenting heat. It made me want to puke.

AK, Stevie and I decided to take our mattress outside and slept under the stars.

Sunday morning arrived and we were back to another day of hard slog clearing the peach trees.

We were running out of beer and we talked AK into driving across the border in the evening to refresh supplies. He was happy to take his Chevy, so at 5p.m. we set off for Oroville, Washington State. We got across to the US alright, bought the beers and went into a hamburger joint with an adjoining bar, where we spent a couple of hours eating and drinking then headed back to Osoyoos, British Columbia. The border customs officers were not the same guys we had seen the previous week. They studied our passports and said to me, 'You guys have come across here both ways recently. What are you up to?'

'Just buying beer,' I replied.

'Oh yeah, no shit?'

'Well yeah, as you know, you can't buy beer in here due to the brewery strike, so as we are only holidaying here in Osoyoos, it's no trouble to come down to Oroville to buy some beers.' Obviously I couldn't say we were gainfully employed on a fruit orchard!

However, the Canadian border guard wasn't buying this. He looked at the three of us very suspiciously.

'OK empty your pockets. We are going to do a little search here, sure hope you haven't got a problem with that.' Looking at his holstered sidearm it didn't seem a good idea to argue with him or his burly colleagues. This was becoming like a scene out of Kojak; hands up against a wall, legs apart while being 'patted down', while another border guard went through our plastic bags containing nothing more than a few food provisions. They went out to the Chevy, looked at the front and rear seats and opened the trunk. AK's car was full of crap and our beers were stashed in the trunk as was legally required. After fifteen minutes, a little chastened and probably a little disappointed, the border security guys said, 'OK you're clean.'

With a little reluctance, our passports were stamped and visas renewed. Our untrusting friend fixed the three of us with a steely stare.

'Don't do this again. Don't go back for more beer. Next time we won't stamp your passports. Got it? Stay out of trouble.'

I didn't know we were in trouble. AK articulated what we all thought, namely that they were convinced we were running drugs over the border, not that they actually said that. However, we got the message and just hoped that we could buy frigging beer in Canada at some point in the future.

We worked a couple more days at the peach farm. On the Tuesday it was nearing 3p.m. finish time when Iron Jaw said, 'I want you guys to do an hour and half overtime.' We all felt too knackered and declined. This definitely didn't please him. The following afternoon we were struggling to clear a particularly large peach tree and could see half a dozen peaches a good fifteen feet in the air, literally just beyond our reach. As Iron Jaw was completely uncompromising we had to clear the tree one way or another. Stevie had a special method to deal with these really awkward buggers when Iron Jaw was out hassling some other unfortunate peach pickers. He used a very long wooden stake designed for propping up the branches, as an enormous baseball bat. Having got a good grip and balance, he took aim and swung the huge pendulum at the offending peach to knock it clean off the tree. Sometimes they came off whole and occasionally they exploded into a mushy shower of shit and rained down on us! Unfortunately on this particular Wednesday afternoon Iron Jaw arrived with calamitous timing just as Stevie hit the peach for a home run. He went berserk:

'That's it – you guys are history. You are all fired as of now. Go clear out your cabin and report to the office tomorrow morning at 9a.m. I'll getcha your paychecks ready for you to collect and I don't wanna see your Limey faces round here no more.'

Suffice to say we found the whole episode hilarious. We had had enough of picking peaches. We were about C$500 better off and ready to leave. AK rather surprised us by saying, 'If you blokes make it to Vancouver Island, look me up. Here's my phone number.' He had never mentioned anything about a home in Vancouver Island before this moment. So much for being a transient on the run; I was getting good at misreading people.

After twelve days we were back on the road again thumbing lifts. It felt good to be standing on the side of the freeway again never quite knowing how long it would take or what surprises might be in store for us.

As it was, it took an hour and a half before we got a lift in an ancient 1947 van. It really was an old heap with bits falling off it and struggling along the open road at 40mph. It did, though, get us two thirds of the way to Vancouver, which was the one good thing about it. It was early evening when we finally arrived in downtown Vancouver and we immediately headed for a youth hostel which had been recommended to us. At just $2 a night it was a bargain and it was good to get our heads down in relative comfort.

One of the addresses Mum had given me was for some distant cousins of hers here in Vancouver. She had written to them upon our departure from home. So the next morning I phoned the Cherry sisters and they were very enthusiastic about meeting Stevie and me. Beattie and Milly were quite elderly but refined ladies who lived together. They were very conservatively dressed in elegant blouses, light cotton cardigans, and tailored skirts below the knee. However, both were sporting dark false eyelashes, which seemed a little out of place and just a bit too long. They reminded me of Endora in *Bewitched*. When they blinked they looked like they were swatting flies. I found this was quite mesmerising and distracting. The sisters were both widowed and empowered, they lived life to the full and were quite engaging. They seemed to be captivated by the two of us as I suspect they had no more idea who we were any more than I knew who they were. All I do know is that we were distantly related – or so my mum said – and that made us family and we were treated as such. During the day, various family

115

members came and introduced themselves. Middle-aged children and teenaged grandchildren and an assortment of first cousins and in-laws all descended on the household to greet us. They organised a huge dinner in our honour. This was middle-class Canada at its best. A middle-aged couple Sue and Andy said, 'You guys come and stay with us for the rest of your time in Vancouver.' God knows what relation they were to me, if any. I just could not work out who was who, maybe one of them was a fourth cousin twice removed or related to the cat, however, they were extremely kind and accommodating.

Over the next few days an array of 'relatives' continued coming to meet us and all insisted on showing us about the Greater Vancouver area and entertaining us at their favourite restaurants. Mass volume eating seemed to be their way of socialising in this part of the world. The restaurants all seemed to be in exotic locations, such as on top of mountains, on river banks, coastal outlooks or swanky downtown premises. The maître-d's and stewards all seemed to know them by name. It was actually a bit embarrassing and somewhat overwhelming. So after three days of hospitality and small talk, almost certainly having put a couple of pounds back on, we said our thank-yous and goodbyes. Andy kindly drove us to Horseshoe Bay where we took a ferry across the Straits of Georgia to Nanaimo, Vancouver Island.

At the port we spotted AK's rusty brown Chevy and

went to his crappy 'Condo' in downtown Nanaimo. It really couldn't have been more different from middle-class Canada, but AK was a straight and honest bloke and still as quiet as a mouse and offered us a choice of the floor or sofa. 'I'm sure you guys have slept on worse.' Too true.

Tuesday 15th August we spent a quiet day in Nanaimo and can't say I thought too much of it. After the Rockies and Vancouver, this was disappointmentville with a capital 'D'. The only saving grace was a British-style pub AK frequented, which was reasonably authentic apart from the beer. It actually sold Double Diamond, but I wasn't going to go there, I considered Molsons to be a safer bet.

AK said his specialty dinner was Chinese.

'Oh that's nice,' cried Steve.

Christ, not more foreign food! It was horrible and I could see that Stevie was revelling in my discomfort as he kept saying to a blank wall how much he was enjoying it. AK was very pleased. I was not!

7. Legover And The Grateful Dead Hangover

Another of my mother's contacts was a good friend of hers called Jenny who immigrated to Victoria a few years ago with her new husband. I had actually met Jenny two or three time in Hastings so remembered her. Mum and Jenny had sung in the Hastings Choral Society Choir together in the early seventies. I had phoned Jenny last night and she came to meet Steve and me at nearby Alberni for coffee and explained she had an assortment of varying commitments, which meant we couldn't stay with her until next Monday 21st, five days from now. This wasn't a problem as we wanted to hitch around the island and take a look.

About midday we parted and started hitching north out of Alberni. Two stunning girls in a bulk standard automobile stopped to give us a lift.

'Say, I just love your accent: you guys from Australia?' asked stunner number one.

As she was quite cute and apparently innocent, I let it ride.

'No, actually we are British.'

We chatted away for half an hour when stunner number two said, 'So where are you guys heading?'

'I don't really know, we have a seen a place on the map called "Pacific Rim National Park" and thought we might take a look up there.'

'Yeah, it is lovely up there. Shall we stop for a beer first if you're in no rush?'

'Sure thing,' piped up Stevie.

We pulled into a bar someplace and we bought the beers. There seemed to be a connection, they were nice girls, but we weren't prepared for what happened next.

'Look if it doesn't matter to you if you go there today, tomorrow or the next day, why don't you come back to Alberni and stay with us.'

Stevie and I, so often on the same wavelength replied in unison, 'Sure thing. Let's go.'

The girls were called Maddison and Lorraine. They stopped off at a liquor store and bought a bottle of Bacardi and a bottle of vodka. Things were getting better all the time. We got back to their apartment and had a few drinks as various other beauties came to join the party. At one point there must have been eight gorgeous women who had all been invited to listen to our British accents and our tales of hitchhiking across Canada. We were a bit of a novelty and we felt like Trophy Brits. We couldn't have cared less, it was like a beauty pageant, every one of them had a magnificent body and they were all absolutely sumptuous and dazzling. They were all a bit of a tease, coming out with loads of sexual innuendos and placing their hands on our knees, chest or behind. Frankly I could have bonked any one of them or ideally the whole damn lot of them. But having taken us to the brink of arousal they suddenly disappeared as fast as they had arrived.

Later the cute but apparently not so innocent Maddison put her arms round me, kissed me and said, 'You don't mind do you?' Stevie and Lorraine had already disappeared. Do I mind? I thought, not at all you divine creature.

119

I was fit to come and virtually threw myself at her. Within seconds we were ripping each other's clothes off and falling onto the settee. We didn't have time to go upstairs; the living room would have to do. After a lot of grunting, panting and squelching, I exploded inside her. My sexual frustration released, we lay calmly beside each other, our arms around each other's bodies in mutual admiration. Frankly if I had died and gone to heaven at that moment it couldn't have been bettered. She was a fantastic lover and I was in ecstasy, and at that precise moment I could have happily stayed in her arms forever.

The next morning, feeling liberated and knackered, we were asked if we would like to stay another night! I kept pinching myself and Stevie couldn't keep the smirk off his face. Stevie told me later I had a pathetic beatific grin all day.

Lorraine said, 'We can show you a few places hereabouts and have lunch at Lorenzo's; Stevie, I want you to meet my best friend, but you'll have to go tomorrow.' Stevie nodded and asked if her best friend was a bloke, much to everybody's enjoyment.

That evening Madison asked when I had last phoned home. I told her I hadn't.

'Oh you really must, surely your mother will be concerned about you. Go on, phone now, help yourself to the phone.' I placed the international trunk call and ten minutes later the operator said, 'Your number is ringing.'

'Hello, Mum.'

'No. Fred.'

'Who the bloody hell is Fred?'

'I think you've got the wrong number, mate,' he growled and hung up.

I was devastated; but Maddie said, 'Look it doesn't matter, try again.' Second time lucky. I was really pleased to talk to Mum. She was a little confused and disorientated, as apparently it was four in the morning in Hastings, but as Maddie said it least I would have put her mind at rest and she would know I was OK.

Stevie said, 'I bet Fed was pleased to answer a wrong number at 4a.m.!'

The next day it was a wrench to leave these two genuinely lovely ladies. They had been fantastic to us on many levels, but they needed to get back to their everyday lives and we wanted to push on. We cadged a lift with a couple from Richmond, Virginia, called Pat and Tom all the way to Long Beach, Pacific Rim National Park. We stopped at a roadside eatery and had soft drinks and sandwiches with Pat and Tom. Before we left, Pat wrote out their address in Richmond and said, 'Come visit us once you guys come back east.'

It was great to see the sea again and for the first time it dawned on me that Stevie and I really had just hitchhiked coast-to-coast, albeit in a snake-like route. And yet if everything was to go to plan, we hadn't even reached the halfway point as yet.

The Pacific Rim was well named, as that was exactly what it was – right on the extreme west coast of Canada. It would be quite a few thousand miles across the Pacific Ocean to the next landmass. In a straight line you would skirt past the northerly tip of Japan and make landfall in Russia a couple of hundred miles north of Vladivostok. Back here in Canada the remote quiet and peaceful Long Beach was a five-mile-long sandy cove with barely a person to be seen.

We had discovered a Vancouver version of Dinty Moore Stew called Puritan Beef Stew, which was certainly no better; we set up the tent and our little gas stove to cook 'dinner'. I don't know if it was the disgusting smell of the stew or our bright green tent but we attracted a group of seriously burnt-out hippies, who seemed to appear from nowhere. They were straight out of the sixties with an average age of thirty-five, they were definitely originals. They were led by a particularly swarthy, disagreeable female with unkempt hair, black fingernails, eyes too close together, overlapping chins and an unmanageable amount of chest. I have always felt women's breasts should never be seen from the rear. I was rather reminded of the great Groucho Marx quip, 'Madam I never forget a face; but in your case I am prepared to make an exception!' Overall they seemed friendly enough though and an interesting collection of dropouts and misfits, the majority was clearly well educated and knowledgeable. They invited us to their 'commune' to hang out, just back off the beach, for a joint and a beer.

The hippie commune looked like an emergency refugee camp in Bangladesh, consisting of about sixty or seventy hippies, tents of all shapes and sizes and a makeshift 'bathroom'. They explained that most summers they arrived here from all over the place to 'hang out' and get away from society. No one knew they were there, therefore lived rent-free and just did what they wanted without recrimination or justification. Free rent and free love, quite a deal. I asked a girl from Minnesota what she was planning on doing this coming winter. She said, 'Well me and some of the other guys are going to head for Egypt next month to see the Grateful Dead in concert at the pyramids. You know the "Dead" don't you?'

I nodded my confirmation, 'Sure I do, "Wake of the Flood" album is one of the finest albums ever recorded. In my view Garcia/Hunter are probably the most underrated songwriters of our times.' That did it for the hippies, I was a fan of the 'Dead' and a British 'Dead Head' at that. They really weren't expecting to me to have heard of them. From that point, Stevie and I were completely accepted and the beer flowed. I tried to keep away from the joints after my Edmonton experience. Someone got a cassette player out and played the brilliant 'American Beauty' album at least three times, while they all snorted their cocaine and got stoned out of their heads on their joints. I thought the Grateful Dead playing the pyramids would be an awesome concert to see and could really appreciate why these guys were so keen to go. How on earth they could afford it I had no idea, but that was none of my business and I didn't ask.

We got back to the tent in the small hours and Stevie, who had been exceptionally quiet all evening, said, 'Shit, what a bunch of arseholes.'

I retorted, 'They were all right, a bit far out maybe, but they're causing no harm to anyone.'

'The bloody "Grateful Dead" more like the "Dreadful Dead". They're crap!'

I couldn't stop laughing. 'There I was thinking you were pining for Lorraine and all the time you were, you despised the "Dead", you poor misguided fool.' I guess they are an acquired taste. And Steve didn't have any.

'Fucking Grateful Dead,' said Stevie and went to sleep and dreamt of Lorraine.

The following morning we hitched north about ten miles to Tofino and on to the picturesque Schooner Cove, where by sheer chance we ran into Pat and Tom from Richmond.

'Hi there, you guys,' shrieked Pat, 'fancy seeing you again so soon.' They said they were staying at a free campsite about a mile away 'so why don't you come up there and set up camp.'

We did just that and spent a very pleasant couple of days exploring the Schooner Cove area and hitching up with the Virginians for red wine and hamburgers each evening.

As we had agreed with Jenny to be in Victoria on Monday, we decided to hitch back down the day before. As luck would have it, it took just one lift all the way back to Nanaimo. We phoned AK and he said, 'The floor and the sofa are still available if you want to stay another night.' Floor or not, AK had been good to us, so we went to his British pub again and bought him something in a basket with French fries and a Molsons as a thank-you.

On Monday, Stevie and I met up with Jenny and her Canadian husband Lawson and they gave us the classic tourist's tour of Victoria. The city was very British in terms of the architecture and nicely laid out. They drove us out to the suburbs to their very genteelly manicured home. I suspected Jenny and her husband, although a lot younger than my mother, were still at least fifteen years older than me and Steve. Jenny was pleasant enough and talked a lot about my mother and Hastings. However, Lawson's body language suggested he wasn't too impressed with us at all. I suspect he thought us a couple of irresponsible undesirables, having a good time and taking every advantage of his wife's generosity. Who's to say he was wrong? However, they didn't have to invite us to their home. No question we probably looked a mess and we had absolutely nothing in common with him whatsoever. He worked in finance and was good at discussing investments, bonds, yields, percentages, returns and dollars. Drawing on my fine command of the Queen's English, I said absolutely nothing; after all there would be no point in asking him if he liked the Grateful Dead, John Mayall's Blues Breakers, a pint of Harveys Best Bitter, cricket or anything else! It was an easy decision to make our excuses and push off the next morning.

The following morning Jenny kindly offered to drive us to the ferry terminal and much to my embarrassment thrust US$100 in my hand, gave me a hug said 'stay safe' and drove off. I was as sure as I could be, Lawson and Jenny had had a row about us being there. Maybe the hundred bucks was a guilt payment or maybe she was genuinely concerned for our welfare. Or as Steve suggested she pinched it from Lawson just to piss him off. I never saw her again; I never found out. We took the ferry to Port Angelis, Washington State. The immigration guys studied our passports and didn't make it easy for us to (re)enter the USA. However, we were becoming quite adept and professional at these border crossing conversations and managed to say all the right things and we were granted a three-month tourist visa.

Highway 101 from the top of Washington state hugs the Pacific coast all the way down to the Mexican border at Tijuana just south of San Diego, California and is nearly as famous as Bob Dylan's 'Highway 61'. We hitched a lift for the first hundred miles of the 101 and pitched the tent by the side of the road just outside a place called Forks, where it proceeded to throw it down all night. The next day we did alright and after a good number of lifts crossed into Oregon. However, it was the third consecutive day of diabolical weather and we made little progress thumbing in the rain. We finished up at a place called Cooes Bay. Our driver, a local, suggested we stay in the Cooes Bay Youth Hostel. We were soaked through and thought maybe it wasn't such a bad idea; we would at least get a shower and clean up. We went to the reception: I can only imagine the receptionist thought we were destitute and waived the fee!

The next day we wanted to get down to the Redwoods, where we were told some of the tallest trees in the world were to be found. A guy at the youth hostel said he would take us there for a couple of bucks, so a little reluctantly we paid him. It was well worth the effort; the trees were enormous and it was a very enjoyable walk. We were told *the* tallest tree in the world was nearby, so set out to find it. Measuring 375 feet tall with a diameter of 59 inches and estimated to be up to eighteen hundred years old, it was a sight to see. These Redwoods *Sequoia Sempervirens* only grow along a 400-mile coastal strip from Oregon down to mid-California. Sadly, logging has wiped out far too many.

The weather had dried up and warmed up and we were only 300 miles short of San Francisco. After three hours' unsuccessfully hitchhiking on the side of the road, Stevie and I agreed to split up and try and make our way to San Francisco separately. This had been something we had discussed back in Vancouver Island. Although we didn't really discuss it we both felt a bit of time away from each other wouldn't be such a bad thing and give us both a little bit of independence and room to breathe. I guess deep down maybe we were getting on each other's nerves. We agreed to meet outside the Frisco General Post Office at midday on Monday 28th August, three days from now.

We stood hitching about a mile apart. A real character in a Mitsubishi pickup truck skidded round a corner into view and screeched to a halt, throwing the driver forward onto his steering wheel.

'Where you heading, dude?' he bellowed.

'Towards Frisco,' I intimated.

'Throw your gear in the back and climb in,' he offered. I accepted.

The driver was a tough-looking character in a torn lumberjack shirt, ripped Levi's and work boots. Although bald, he had long greasy hair round the sides tied back into a pony tail. He was a bit of an oddball, but said he had majored in world economics – whatever world economics is – and worked in social care. The guy was another great example of never judging people by appearance. We chatted a while and gave him a thumbnail outline of the last few weeks, then casually I asked if he had passed a guy in a red windcheater and stubbly beard back there. He said, 'I sure did and drove right on past him.' I laughed and told him who he was. The guy slammed on the brakes and spun the pickup round in one sweeping move.

'If that dude back there is your buddy, let's go get him.' I didn't have the heart to ask him not to. We drove back five miles and sure enough Stevie was still thumbing a ride.

Our oddball social worker said his name was Hal Riggs and lived in a place with the unusual name of Eureka on the Pacific coast. As it happened Eureka was by American standards quite an old town, having first been settled by the white man in the 1850s. Some of the original buildings from the period still exist today. Hal invited us to stay for the night at his house, which we were happy to agree to. We got to a very normal house to be greeted by his very normal-looking wife and three young very noisy kids.

Hal said, 'Let's go out and have a beer and some peace and quiet.' We went to a quiet bar and had a couple of beers and rather indiscreetly mentioned his lifestyle and character came across as rather contradictory. This didn't offend Hal one bit. He said he lived by the following creed:

'I have four rules to follow for a happy life with women. One, it's important to have a woman who helps at home, does the cooking and tidies up. Secondly, it is important to have a woman who can make you laugh, that you can trust and is straight with you. Third, it is very important to be with a woman who is good in bed and can satisfy your every desire. Fourth and last, it is vitally important these three women should never meet!'

I don't think we stopped laughing for five minutes. Hal sat there with his beer with a deadpan face as if he really meant it, which made it funnier still.

About 10p.m. he asked if we were hungry. We said we could eat and to our amusement he said, 'Let's go to WinCo Grocery store.' He walked us to the rear of the store where there was a small queue of the local 'down-and-outs'. The store manager was handing out food and produce to the needy. I wasn't sure we qualified, but Hal said, 'You let me take care of this' and came away with enough food to feed a small army. 'We call this "Fresh Garbage", WinCo give away surplus out-of-date food, five days a week. I come here once or twice most weeks to take stuff home to the kids.' I couldn't really work Hal out. He seemed to have a job and stable home life and yet he was an oddball who could be extremely funny, who had discovered a very cost-effective, if not entirely ethical, method of feeding his family for free.

Back at the house he said, 'You guys will have to sleep in the cellar.'

He opened up a trapdoor in the hall floor and gave us a 'flashlight'.

'Oh, there is no lighting down there, just take your sleeping bags and I'll see you in the morning.' It was like the Black Hole of Calcutta down there. If Hal didn't come to open up the hall floor trapdoor tomorrow morning we could die down there and never be discovered. Fortunately Hal's Mrs did open it up at nine the next morning and invited us to a very conventional breakfast. The normality of breakfast was another contradiction in their lifestyle.

We hit the road mid-morning and a lady in a jeep pulled in for us. She looked like a middle-aged version of Jayne, my 'girlfriend from the year before' (to quote Paul Simon), although somewhat more liberal, Californian style. She suggested a detour via Shelter Cove, Humboldt County. She drove off the 101 and waxed lyrical about the beauty of Shelter Cove. It was pleasant enough but certainly nothing out of the ordinary on this coastline of outstanding scenery.

Having wasted nearly three hours' travelling time, she dropped us at a place called Garberville, barely sixty miles south of Eureka and there we stayed. We hitched for four and half hours without a sniff of success. We gave up, wandered across a field and set up the tent behind a shack out of view of the road and then wandered back to see if we could find a bar and some grub. In less than a mile we came across a place which served our purposes. We got a few strange looks until we opened our mouths and the drinkers realised we weren't from around these parts. A guy sidled over to us and said, 'Shit, we thought you were with those biker fellas down the street.'

'Nope we don't own a bike or a leather jacket,' Stevie confirmed. 'So who are they then?'

'Fucking Hell's Angels, that's who. They come up here from Frisco, Oakland, Sacramento and San Jose and all over to drink and do drugs and cause trouble and shit. They piss in the street, steal from the stores, terrorise decent folk on their bikes and make a hellava mess, leaving all their shit and stuff everywhere. The police sort of have them contained over at the Big R, but they have their work cut out.'

Christ, no wonder we couldn't get a lift, I thought. 'How many of them are there?' I asked.

'Gotta be two hundred. They won't cause any trouble in here; Billy there would blow their brains out if they cause any shit.' Billy was the owner of the bar and stood 6'6" tall and tapped a shotgun he kept behind the bar. This was like something out of the Wild West. I nodded, scoffed my burger, knocked back my beer and just wanted to get out of there. We got back to the tent and just hoped we were far enough out of town to remain undetected and undisturbed.

The next day was a Sunday so we decided to take our chances and start early and hope all the Hells Angels were too crashed out to worry about us. Thankfully we got lucky and managed a lift within ten minutes, much to our relief. We were driven 150 miles towards San Francisco, leaving us just fifty miles short, which we achieved in a couple of easy lifts.

It was obvious we couldn't pitch a tent in San Francisco so we tried to book in to the local youth hostel only to find it full.

'Come back tomorrow,' the guy said. 'Mondays is always the quietest day in here.' We said we would and went off to look for a cheap hotel for the night. We found a dump called the Windsor. The weirdo behind the counter came from an alternative universe; his greasy hair was all over the place and wrapped in a red bandanna which only inflated the turgidity of his unkempt image. He was covered in African-style beads, an assortment of chain necklaces and bracelets and leather straps, he wore a collarless shirt undone to his navel and his trousers looked more like floral pyjama bottoms than not. His name was Vince and he ripped us off, insisting on $7 up front. I just looked him in the eye and said, 'Hey man, far out.' Vince the weirdo was too spaced out to appreciate irony. I handed over seven $1 bills. The Windsor was the absolute pits, full of losers and loners. The wallpaper was peeling off the walls, it smelt musty and dirty and the rooms were as basic as could be. I didn't fancy using the twenty-year-old worn-out nylon sheets so unfurled my sleeping bag.

After a bit of a kip we ventured out into downtown Frisco at sun fall. The vibrancy of the city hit me like a smack in the gob! The streets were alive with neon, smelly burger joints, porn shops and prostitutes; it was both ghastly and glorious. There were dropouts and druggies, perverts and transvestites, tramps and freaks, cranks and loonies, dossers and queers and all colours and creeds, all in one big intermingling amalgam of a kaleidoscopic pastiche, blended in a melting pot medley – or something like that! My Hastings College of Further Education experience had not prepared me for such a heuristic encounter. It wasn't like this in St Leonards-on-Sea! I was absolutely flabbergasted and stupefied with amazement. Stevie had seen all this last year and knew exactly what to expect; he thought my reaction was very funny and admitted his reaction had been exactly the same first time round. 'You just had to see it to believe it,' he said.

'I've seen it and I am not sure I do believe it.'

The next day we checked out of the abhorrent Windsor Hotel, where despite some very arduous and formidable competition, I was convinced that Vince was my winner of the Richard Wynter 'Weirdo of the Year Award'! We made straight for the youth hostel, where we checked-in our backpacks into a padlocked cupboard. We then made our way down to Fisherman's Wharf and took a ferry across to Sausalito and caught a good glimpse of Alcatraz, the abandoned prison Island in the Bay. We then walked back across the Golden Gate Bridge to the city. The Golden Gate was without question a big tick in the box, as I had seen this American icon so many times on TV and in *Dirty Harry* movies etc. Halfway across we stopped for a slash over the side in celebration of the achievement. Of course Mother Nature had her own back and blew the long chain of piss back all over us!

Back in town we went on one of the famous streetcars up and down the steep San Francisco Avenues. They are at least sixty years old, if not more. They thundered down the steep slopes towards the next intersections. The brake man has to pull the vast levers backwards to bring the cars to a stop. They put everything into it and never look as though they are going to make it but miraculously they do and shudder to a halt at the red lights, thereby avoiding catastrophic collisions.

We returned to the hostel by 8p.m. and found that half the residents were British and the other half Continental European. We got talking to four lads from Keswick, Cumbria and went out to a sleazy bar with them for a few beers. Somehow I just couldn't find the women in there appealing; I just felt it was too dodgy. I didn't know where they had been and I certainly wasn't going to pay for it. The sleaze just put me right off so I went back to the hostel and had a good night's sleep. I am fairly sure everyone else took the same view.

The time-worn hippies back at Pacific Rim National Park had strongly advised Stevie and me to go to the Haight-Ashbury District of Frisco, where reputedly the whole Flower Power movement started back in the sixties. Because of my love of music and a lot of the bands I enjoyed had their roots in the sixties' counter culture of psychedelia, I was keen to see what was reputed to be the epicentre of the 1967 Summer of Love and the Flower Power movement.

Of course in 1967 I was far too young at ten years

old to appreciate the colossal social and cultural changes, the liberal use of LSD, sexual permissiveness, the protest against the Vietnam War. I wouldn't have known about any of that and definitely would not have known where Vietnam was in the world or what the war was about and nor did a lot of the young American boys sent to out to fight and die, which culminated in the mass peaceful protests against the pointless slaughter. The only thing I could remember about 1967 was Sergeant Pepper's Lonely Heart Club Band and a ten-year-old girl called Gillian Magee, my first crush!

So Stevie and I found ourselves at a fairly anonymous-looking intersection where once upon a time 100,000 people had gathered in protest, worn flowers in their hair and listened to such groups as the Jefferson Airplane, The Mamas & The Papas, Scot McKenzie, Janis Joplin, the Flower Pot Men and of course the Grateful Dead, all of whom were spawned out of San Francisco Bay area. Today it looked what it was, a fairly typical Frisco suburb with a little evidence of what went before just eleven years ago. There was a small souvenir shop selling posters, LPs, beads and bells, mementoes and Afghan coats, while Jefferson Airplane's 'White Rabbit' played in the background. We stood at the intersection and tried to breathe in the sixties vibe, but it wasn't there for us, so we went to McDonald's instead.

8.   The Half Dome Calamity Into The Valley Of Death

Both Stevie and the Reverend had mentioned Guy and Herbie a few times before we left home and over the last couple of months. Stevie had spent time with them in 1977 and now decided to ring them as we were not so far from Redwood City. Stevie said Guy was working at a place called the Great American Parkway at Santa Clara. Guy had a big job, project managing the 'GAP'. It was in essence a very large theme park with attractions, rides and a circus. Guy invited us over and said to go to the box office and ask for an envelope in Steve Elder's name. We made our way to Santa Clara and found the GAP very easily. Inside the envelope was a book of tickets for the rides and direction to Guy's office. Steve said he wasn't doing this last year, but recalled Guy did work on a self-employed basis in management specialising in the entertainment business.

Guy jumped up from behind a desk and slapped Stevie on the back.

'Gee, it is great to see you again.' Stevie introduced me.

'So, Richard, you're here in place of Marcus.'

I told Guy that Marcus was working in London and that I had persuaded Stevie to give it another go and I was loving every minute of it.

'I know why Stevie is back here in California so soon,' he said with a smile. 'You want to see Rachael again, I'm sure.' I thought I saw Stevie actually blush. 'She's still down in San Diego if you're heading down that way. Stevie indicated it was very much on his list of people and places to visit but explained we were keeping things flexible as we didn't like being tied down to any exacting schedule.

Guy was terrific; he showed us around a bit and opened a few doors not available to the general public, before returning to his desk. The rides were like nothing I had ever seen at a British funfair, they had enormous rollercoasters and a 360-degree loop known as the 'Tidal Wave'. The best we got in Hastings was the Octopus, Waltzer, Dodgems and Big Wheel, which barely reached above the rooftop, plus a coconut shy! This was on a different level altogether. GAP also had two outdoor massive movie screens for evening 'drive-in' movies and a stage show where various comedians and crooners appeared.

We had a great time enjoying ourselves without costing us a cent. At nine in the evening we hooked up with Guy who drove to his home in Redwood City. Guy's house was a large four-bedroom one-level detached property. Tastefully decorated although somewhat sparsely furnished, it did contain a large TV set and a state-of-the-art Hi Fi system and an assortment of self-assembly furniture. Outside there was a small orange orchard, well-tended garden, obligatory basketball ring and a swimming pool. Herbie seemed to be no more and Guy made no reference to him, so Stevie thought it best not to ask. We ate 'submarines', which were foot-long bread rolls full of meats, salad and avocado. Guy said, 'Look I have to go to a meeting tomorrow in LA but you guys are very welcome to stay here, use the pool, make yourself at home and relax. If the flights run to time I will be back by eight.'

After the hustle and bustle and sheer frenzy of Frisco, it was actually quite nice to take a 'day off' and not do too much. It was also nice to take a day away from tents, hostels and communes. Guy had a collection of Joni Mitchell albums. Apart from 'Big Yellow Taxi' I didn't know much about her music. I had to admit sitting by the pool listening to Joni's music quietly wafting in the background was one of the most relaxing experiences of my life. I made a note of a couple of her albums I would buy when I returned home. Stevie as ever had the last word and said, 'I think I preferred the Dreadful Dead.' Philistine! He just lacked any real appreciation of quality music.

Friday September 1st, we agreed with Guy to meet up again in a few weeks at his other place in Redlands and he drove out to the interstate and we started hitching to Yosemite National Park. We made excellent progress and made the outskirts of Yosemite by dusk. Our last lift was with a bloke who was a bit of a pisshead and linked up with a druggie pal of his and the four of us went to a poxy open-air party in a field nearby. We were close enough to where we wanted to be, so sneaked away from the party, walked a mile in the dark and pitched the tent in wooded area. After an hour we were awoken by a raccoon stealing our food. We were not amused. However, we were amused to find the next morning we were actually beside one of the main car parks for Yosemite National Park.

We spent two hours in Yosemite Village where we washed, ate and deposited part of our gear, including the tent, into lockers. It was very warm and with no rain forecast we were happy to sleep out under the stars. We bought a 24-hour permit which included the 'Half Dome'. We set out on what our guide map said was an 8.2 mile hike to the top of Half Dome. Our backpacks were 15–20 pounds lighter but it was still a gruelling hike. It was incredibly steep all the way and we both found it harder than the Grand Tetons. Dave Kiln would have been proud of us. We stopped for a rest and a drink of water every twenty minutes. We reached a flattish area half a mile from the top and decided to secure our food and belongings over a tree branch. At this point a fella joined us and said his name was Ramesh Chandra. He was an Indian, originally from Maharashtra, but became a naturalised American ten years ago. He also secured his belongs over a separate tree branch. I liked Ramesh as we had a lot in common, not least cricket and Yosemite. Sadly he had never heard of the Grateful Dead!

We staggered up the last half a mile to the top at 8500 feet. I was a little disappointed at the top after such an immense effort as the view was blanked out by the clouds. The top was as its name suggested just a large bare granite dome devoid of foliage. We returned to our base camp at dusk and set about a feast of Dinty Moore Stew and cheese sandwiches and Indian black tea. About 10p.m., now lying in our sleeping bags in the pitch black, we heard a loud crack. A bear had found our tree and was doing his best to bring down the branch. Ramesh had a power torch (or flashlight as the Americans prefer to call them) and scanned the area to our left. A row of bright yellow eyes reflected back at us. Ramesh looked alarmed and said with a thick Indian accent 'Oh bloody hell' while nodding his head from side to side in that unique Indian style, which despite the seriousness of the situation made me laugh. We calculated there had to be at least five bears. We made an instant decision and banged our saucepans together and yelled at them at the top of our voices. It made no difference; they were approaching us and wouldn't be put off. I felt as threatened as Lieutenant John Chard at Rorke's Drift as the Zulu warriors closed in. Unlike the brave Lieutenant, I followed Stevie's advice.

'Fuck this,' he screamed. 'Let's get out of here.' My sentiments exactly.

We were all on the same wavelength and grabbed our sleeping bags, abandoning all other possessions, and ran back up the Half Dome with Ramesh leading the way with his power torch. We knew the bears weren't interested in us, but the lure of the remains of Dinty Moore Stew was something of an attraction to the family of bears. I don't deny it was a scary moment and we decided to stay put at the top of the Dome for our own safety until morning. The bears were welcome to Dinty Moore! It was bloody freezing up there and suffice to say we did not sleep at all well. Just after dawn we clambered back down to retrieve what was left of our belongings. The bears had somehow managed to bring the branch down, which was a good 25 foot above the ground and ripped open one of the back packs and shaken everything out. The stove and pots had been kicked about and licked clean. All our remaining food had gone, a couple of shirts and T-shirts had been strewn about. Fortunately most things were usable so we collected everything together and made our way back down to Yosemite Village, all 8.2 miles of it.

It was almost harder going back down as my legs ached so much from yesterday's effort. We collected the rest of our gear and found a shower block to refresh and clean up. We decided against buying more food from the 'supply store' as apart from the fact it was well overpriced, we had been robbed by both raccoons and bears over the past two nights and saw little point in giving them yet another opportunity to eat at our expense. So we bought a 6oz cheeseburger and fries and a bottle of water to take away. It was still light, but still feeling knackered Stevie and I had no desire to go too far. We decided to head back to the wooded area by the car park where we slept two nights ago and have an 'early night'.

About seven the next morning we were awoken by a park warden who delighted in telling us we were camping illegally and without a permit.

'I will be back in fifteen minutes and you had better be gone or else you're gonna get a big fine.' We scarpered double quick!

We hitchhiked out of Yosemite through the Tioga Pass, the highest pass in the Sierra Nevada and indeed in all California; it was really something to behold. We were heading for a 'ghost town' called Bodie, which Ramesh recommended. We got a lift with two women and their teenage sons. Bodie was amazing; I thought it was a Hollywood mock-up for making cowboy films, but in fact it is a genuine abandoned town, built in the 1870s and at one point during the gold rush had a population of some 7500 people. As soon as the gold disappeared the people disappeared too and by 1893 there was no one left. Unfortunately, while we were there, it started to rain quite hard, which was a real shame. We would have liked to explore more but there was virtually no shelter and we really didn't fancy a drenching. The good ladies and sons kindly picked us up again and drove on an unmade road in the mist and rain and nearly hit a cow standing on the side of the road as the visibility was so poor. We stopped off at some two-bit shit hole and had a bowl of piss-poor soup and cold coffee. The rain was getting worse. We were miles from nowhere, a good 7000 feet above sea level, cold, wet and fairly hungry. It all felt a bit depressing. The ladies took pity on us and said, 'OK we are renting a holiday condo down the road; the two boys can bunk together and you two guys can bunk together in one of their rooms.' I don't think I had ever felt so grateful. The ladies at last introduced themselves as Jeanie and Lola from LA. They were on their annual vacation. We told them we were planning on going to Death Valley. Regrettably the next day it was still raining, the man on the TV said 'Storm Norman' was going to take a day or two to pass through and that flash floods were to be expected. This really put the kybosh on our plans. Jeanie said, 'We are driving back to LA today, so if you guys want to come with us you are welcome to a lift the whole way.'

As ever our plans were fluid and we thought why not, let's see Los Angeles. On the way I checked my mum and dad's many contacts list and found a cousin on Mum's side with an LA address. When Lola stopped for a natural break, I used a pay phone and rang Dick and Barbara Kaste. Barbara was a first cousin of my mother's and therefore of mine, once removed, as I understand it. They were more than a little flabbergasted to hear from me, but she said, 'You two come right on over.' I explained we were a few hundred miles out, but would be there sometime this evening.

It was a 350-mile journey before Lola dropped us off the interstate near Saugus and I knocked on Dick and Barbara's door. A huge man towering a good eight to nine inches over me (and I am virtually 6' tall) wearing a cheesecloth shirt, chinos and cowboy boots answered the door and said, 'Well you just gotta be Babs' British relations. Babs has had to go out this evening, but I'm gonna take you out to dinner right now. Hope you guys are hungry.'

As knackered as we felt after 350 miles and really in need of a good shower, we jumped in Dick's car and set off to the Saugus Café, which Dick explained is the oldest café in California and one of the oldest in the USA. I thought maybe if it is that old and important it might be real plush and grand in there. It wasn't! It was, however, an old school American diner with a half-decent menu. 'You guys have anything you want,' insisted Dick. We were more than a bit hungry and demolished a 12oz T-bone steak each. Dick was good company and knew far more about my mother than I thought he would. As with all the other relations in North America they had never met.

After a while, Dick surprised me by saying, 'I've booked you guys a twin room at a hotel.' Again American hospitality embarrassed us. He mumbled something about their home being untidy and junk in the spare room or such like. I tried to explain we had spent three-and-a-half months sleeping in fields and roadsides every other night and it didn't matter, but he insisted the room was booked and drove us to the Howard Johnson at a place called Birbank. 'Look I won't be here to collect you guys until midday tomorrow, so enjoy yourselves; the account is all taken care of.'

We were staying at a high-end swish hotel, all expenses paid. Dick had booked the room and breakfast but said 'put anything else you want on the tab'. We thought putting drinks on the room would be taking the piss, so having not spent more than a dollar fifty all day, we bought a few beers at the bar and couldn't believe our good fortune.

The room was a smart en suite with tasteful décor with two large single beds. The furnishings included a desk with drawers, shelves and cupboard, ironing-board press, mini bar, room fan and a good-sized television. We leant our backpacks against the cupboard, threw our pongy clothes into a laundry bag; we had landed on our feet again. After an excellent night's sleep and first-class buffet breakfast, Stevie put the TV on. We sat there on our beds for two hours watching morning TV, just to be American. A copy of the room bill had been slid under our door

144

and I was shocked to see a bill of $48 for our stay, including $6 for the laundry. In our naivety we thought it was free!

Bang on twelve, Dick and Barbara and their son Brett arrived. Barbara was a striking middle aged woman with a bubbly personality and charm. Young Brett was rake thin, bespectacled, an almost delicate lad of about sixteen, who had a face as long and pale as a rasher of streaky bacon, and about as devoid of expression. I wondered if he had been adopted.

We sat down had coffee and made formal introductions. Dick excused himself and said, 'I'll see you tonight at home.' Barbara firmly stated. 'Right we are going to the Magic Mountain fun park this afternoon.' As with most things and places in this part of the world, I had never heard of Magic Mountain or knew what to expect. We arrived at an enormous 'fun park'. It was maybe twice the size of the Great American Parkway, but without the cinemas, stage shows and circus. It was a funfair to end all funfairs! The centre piece was the largest and the fastest roller coaster in the world called the 'Colossus'. And it certainly was. It had two one-hundred-foot drops and the g-force on some of the bends was quite sensational. Barbara or 'Babs' now made me blush again when she bought us a book of tickets each and wouldn't accept any payment from us. She said, 'You two do your own thing and meet us back here at five o'clock. Brett and I have been here many times, we're gonna visit friends.'

We were so blown away by the Colossus we went on it twice, even though we had to 'wait in line' for over an hour both times.

That evening we were to stay at the Kaste household, which had been cleaned from top to bottom and given a good makeover. I don't know if they thought we were royalty but they really pulled out all the stops for us, much to my continued mortification; I felt unworthy and a fraud. Stevie as ever brought in his unique brand of humour and said 'They only have to look at us and then look at the hotel bill to realise we're not worth it!'

While Babs was preparing an all-American dinner in the kitchen, we saw Brett blow-drying his bouffant hair with a large electric handheld hairdryer. Stevie closed the bedroom door and said to me with a very serious face, 'I really think that lad is of dubious sexuality.' I nearly cried with laughter.

We ate a traditional US dinner of meatloaf, with a side dish of 'tater tots' followed by apple pie; it was quite wonderful. Babs asked if we would like tea. She served it black, so I asked for milk. Brett excelled himself.

'I never heard of milk in tea before,' he whined. This kid was starting to bug me; in fact I was shocked at his ignorance, so I calmly told him. 'I come from the biggest tea-drinking nation in the world, where drinking tea is a national pastime and very much a part of British culture. The vast majority of Brits drink their tea with milk,' I emphasised.

'Oh,' he said with a hint of a glare and walked out.

I don't know what it was about Cousin Brett, but

he had one of those faces you just want to slap! Dick, sensing my slight annoyance with his half dimwit son, strode over to his drinks cabinet and pulled out a full bottle of Kentucky bourbon. 'Personally I would put this in it,' he roared. That broke the ice and restored harmony. Two hours later the bottle was now seriously depleted, Dick and Babs were well gone, closely followed by me and Stevie. As with so many of the folk we had visited over the past few months they were just terrific company and we got on like a house on fire.

Thursday 7th September we had decided to try again to hitch to Death Valley, which was due west of Saugus just over the Nevada state border. We made it to the main Death Valley junction by 4p.m. but struggled for three hours to thumb a lift the last twenty-five miles, until a couple of Froggies far from home stopped and took us right in to the heart of the Valley to a place called Furnace Creek. We went to the one and only bar, the Creek Bar, the only bar within a hundred miles, had a pitcher of beer and bought as much water as we could carry with us. There was a free campsite, but it was far too hot for a tent so we crashed out, lying on a couple of picnic tables hoping to avoid the scorpions and snakes.

After a fairly uncomfortable night's sleep we dumped our backpacks at the visitor centre and tried to hitch north to see the sand dunes. It was hopeless and after two and half hours gave up and hitched south towards the desert and the salt pans. It was stifling hot and we were pouring sweat. The sun was too bright and shiny, the sky was too blue and the distant heat haze was shimmering too sharply. The road tarmac was melting and the shadows too short. Even the cacti were wearing sunglasses.

A warden in aviator shades, in a four-wheel-drive Jeep stopped and just stared at us for about thirty seconds. He seemed lost for words and then suddenly exploded.

'ARE YOU FUCKING MAD?'

'What?' Stevie mumbled.

'What the hell do you guys think you are doing?'

'Hitching,' I flippantly replied.

'For Christ's sake don't you know, you guys, you could die of thirst out here in just four hours without water?' I showed him my water bottle.

'Get in,' he barked.

Our aviator warden looked as though he should have been a prison guard keeping watch on the chain gang – maybe he had been once upon a time – and introduced himself as Roger. Making the usual assumption we were Australian he said, 'You probably don't understand the seriousness of the heat and dehydration out here.' Had we been Australian we probably would have, but couldn't be bothered to tell him we were Limeys from East Sussex. However, Roger said he was 'doing his rounds' which involved driving a good sixty-mile circuit around the southern part of Death Valley through the desert and the salt pans, which may have involved looking out for stranded Australians and other unfortunates.

The 'salt pans' were yet another strange quirk of nature. As the sea receded and evaporated many millions of years ago it left huge quantities of salt deposits in large jagged clusters. Roger started to enjoy his role as tour guide and pointed out various things of interest and said, 'Right here at the Badwater Basin we are 282 feet below sea level, the lowest elevation in North America.' After four hours he dropped us back at Furnace Creek where Roger informed us it was at this exact point the highest world air temperature ever to be recorded, on 10th July 1913, was of some 134 degrees. 'And remember, guys, that temperature is taken in the shade.' But get this; it is also the place of the highest recorded surface temperature of 201 degrees Fahrenheit just six years ago! The only time in world history the surface temperature had risen above 200 degrees. It didn't feel too far off a world record today either, it was unbelievably hot. We went for a swim at the hotel pool to cool off and then for a beer before retrieving our gear and heading back to the campsite. Tonight we suffered yet another can of Dinty Moore Stew and wondered if we were anywhere close to setting a world record for consumption of this revolting fodder.

The following morning, despite Roger's sensible warning, we hitched north again as we were determined to see the sand dunes. We got a lift to a way-station called Stovepipe Wells and from there we walked a mile to see Mosaic Canyon, which was quite beautiful. We then walked a further couple of miles to the sand dunes. They were quite incredible and well worth the effort, which was not inconsiderable. By Sahara Desert standards these dunes are tiny, but nonetheless captivating and enchanting. The shadowy ripple effects the winds create in the sand are quite mesmerising. They were not particularly tall or steep but trying to walk up them in the ceaseless sun with the sand constantly giving way under your feet was a challenge of daring and dedication. Many would say stupidity. Maybe; but we did it.

Back at Furnace Creek we placed a note on a notice board requesting a lift to Las Vegas for the following day. After a while a German couple approached us and got talking. I thought by the way the conversation was going, they had come to let us know they were not going to Vegas tomorrow – which they weren't! However, they were interesting enough company and we repaired to the 'Creek Bar' for a pitcher or two of beer. We eventually reached seven pitchers between us and slept very soundly on our tabletops!

After a good swim in the hotel pool and a shower and a light breakfast in the hotel restaurant, we were lucky to hitch to Las Vegas in less than three hours, arriving around 4.30 in the afternoon. Our driver dropped us near to the Greyhound station, so we deposited our gear in a luggage locker and took a look around town. I guess it doesn't matter how often you see places like Las Vegas on TV and the movies, it still is quite an experience to actually be there. There were amazing casinos absolutely everywhere, very cheap food and other attractions to entice you in to part with your money. We were offered free photographs, free phone calls 'anywhere in the USA' and free drinks. We phoned Barbara and Dick to thank them once more for their hospitality and ate whatever we could lay our hands on. With a $3-a-day limit we could not afford to gamble; however, we decided to get a dollar's worth of dimes each to waste away, just to have gambled in Vegas and tick another box. At 9p.m. we caught a bus to the 'Strip', home to the Sands, Golden Nugget, the Dunes and Caesars Palace to see what all the fuss was all about. The razzmatazz went up another level; every casino was covered in colour-changing neon lighting which I found absolutely fascinating. I also found it more than a bit tacky and it was sad to see people gamble away vast quantities of cash on fruit machines that were obviously fixed to pay out once in a blue moon. The roulette wheels and crab tables also were stacked against them. There wasn't a chance in hell of recovering their losses. And yet people were falling over themselves to throw their money away. By two in the morning with Vegas in full swing and the thermometer still up in the nineties, we made our way back to the Greyhound station to collect our backpacks. We strode off to find a place behind a plush hotel to lie down; we unfurled our tent and laid it on the sand and used it as a ground sheet, and fell asleep in the warm desert air.

After just five hours' sleep we awoke by the glaring sun and building heat and went into the hotel to use the facilities. The machines and tables were still going strong. Vegas was a 24-hour-a-day business. Breakfast was free and we bunged a hotel croupier a dollar to let us use a shower. It took a few hours to get a decent lift out of Vegas but a Dutch couple stopped for us and said they were going to the Grand

Canyon. That was fine by us, we wanted to go there too!

9.   Canyons, Monuments And The Man On The Moon

We had asked our hosts to drop us a few miles short of the Canyon as we didn't want to pay out for a campsite, and literally threw our tent up on the side of the road and fell asleep. The last thirty-six hours in Vegas had caught up with us and we slept undisturbed for ten-and-a-half hours! All we had was water and a biscuit for breakfast, but that was fine. As soon as we were ready and packed, we stuck our thumbs out and the very first vehicle to come along pulled over and took us the final seven miles to Grand Canyon National Park visitor centre. We decided on a quiet day and wrote letters home, bought lunch and did some laundry. For security we decided again it would be better to leave most of our gear in a secure locker at the visitor centre and went for a mile-or-two stroll around the rim of the Canyon. The Grand Canyon is one of the deepest gorges in the world; its rock stratas, colours and geological formations are phenomenal. As the sun moves round or creeps behind the clouds, the colours change and images of the canyon seems to shift. No wonder millions of people visit the canyon every year; it is one of the great natural wonders of the world. At the very base the Colorado River cuts through, winding itself through rapids and its many tributaries. The views are as captivating as they are hypnotic.

Early evening we were directed to a campsite and met up with a Rhodesian fella and his Irish girlfriend. We agreed to share a pitch with them to reduce the fee by half. We had a basic meal of cold meats and salad and drank a few beers. It was a nice quiet relaxing evening with a bit of banter and good humour. I was very confused by the time, as my watch had stopped. In Nevada we had been on Pacific time, while here in Arizona we were on Mountain time but there was also daylight saving time here so I had no idea what it was and nor did anyone else. I decided to go by own 'Richie time' zone, because frankly it really didn't matter what the time was!

The following day Stevie and I went on a very long and exhilarating hike right down into the depths of the Canyon. We hiked four-and-a-half miles down the outer canyon then a further mile-and-a-half across the plateau. Yet again the views and vista were absolutely stunning, it really did take your breath away. It was incredibly hot on the plateau. Looking at the river from the plateau and back up the slopes of the Canyon overwhelmed the senses. It gave me an incredible feeling of insignificance. The sheer depth of the gorge was astonishing. We had walked six miles in four-and-a-half hours and we were still a good couple of miles from the river. As much as we would have liked to have reached the bottom it was going to be impossible given the sheer scale and distance. We also had to factor in our energy levels and the time it would take to return. So with some reluctance we decided to head back up. We reached the top, having hiked route one in just over two hours. I cannot deny we were pleased with ourselves for hiking a route most tourists didn't attempt, although plenty went by Donkey!

To celebrate we decided to splash out on a decent meal at a quality restaurant adjoining the visitor centre. While waiting for a table we got talking to a very well-to-do English lady from Beaconsfield; she seemed utterly beguiled and dumbfounded by our achievement today and also our journey by thumb from New York over the past four months. Her name was called and she was escorted to her table. For once we thought bollocks to the cost, we hadn't eaten properly since Las Vegas so let's just enjoy ourselves eat well and make merry. As it turned out this was probably the best meal we had eaten in those four months – a shrimp starter, granary rolls and butter, followed by a large fillet steak and chips, side salad, cheesecake, Californian red wine and coffee. We even bought a cigar each at the end of the feast and we didn't smoke! Stevie asked the waiter for the bill and he said it was all paid for by the English lady who had just left. We ran out of the restaurant to thank her but she had gone, never to be seen again. For once we were truly humbled; we were complete strangers and had only spoken with her for ten minutes. Both Steve and I were incredibly grateful. It was just a shame we didn't know her name or who she was, it was an extraordinarily charitable and munificent act of human kindness.

With our bellies full of good food and wine we had another sound night's sleep and decided to have one last look at the Canyon from a viewing platform a mile or so along the rim before moving on. While on the platform, an elderly couple spotted I was wearing a blue (now-faded) Sussex County Cricket Club T-shirt proudly displaying the Sussex Martlet crest. He said he was from Horsham and a Sussex supporter. He went on to say Sussex had won the Gillette Cup at Lords just twelve days before and had gone to the match. I was of course delighted my club had actually won something. I knew they had reached the semi-final stage, but I was jubilant at *my* club's success; quite fantastic. They had beaten a strong Somerset side with Ian Botham, Viv Richards and Joel Garner – fresh out of the Canadian second XI league. Sussex had quite a young side – Greig and Snow had moved on – without many household names, apart from the great Imran Khan. I was ecstatic. Stevie as ever showed total disinterest and said 'Oh!'

One of the things that had drawn me to the USA was the Wild West. I had been brought up on a plethora of Westerns, cowboy and Indian films with John Wayne, James Stewart, Kirk Douglas, Robert Taylor and the brilliant Clint Eastwood. It wasn't only the star qualities of these great characters but the rugged landscapes. Nothing typified it more than a backdrop of peculiar monoliths and buttes standing hundreds of feet high out of the desert plains. Reading from a book on the 'Great American Country' I had studied in a Grand Canyon souvenir shop, this classic western landscape was called Monument Valley and it was only 175 miles north-east of our current position, right on the border of Utah and Arizona. I absolutely had to go there.

We left Grand Canyon National Park after lunch and were fortunate to thumb a couple of decent lifts the majority of the route. Our last lift was with an indigenous Red Indian fella who told us it was would be extremely difficult to hitch around Monument Valley as due in no small part to a lack of traffic, but more importantly in his view, as the whole of the Monument Valley area was a protected Navajo Indian Reservation and was not a designated National Park. He dropped us off at an Indian village called Kayenta about twenty miles from Monument Valley at 9p.m. The settlement was certainly very different to the vast majority of places we had been through.

I wasn't particularly well versed in modern Red Indian society; I was certainly aware that generally Americans, black or white, didn't hold the Indians in high esteem and generally looked down on them and probably still considered them a nuisance and irritation, but of course the days of cowboys and Indians was long gone. Massacres and scalpings were way in the past and an uneasy alliance had been agreed.

Back in Eureka, I recall Hal Riggs talking about American Indians as he had a few pals of Native Indian heritage and was subsequently quite knowledgeable on the subject. He told us Indians had lived and hunted in mainland America for at least fifteen thousand years. The white man had brutally massacred large numbers, but the diseases they brought from Europe played a much larger part. It is estimated in the eighteenth and nineteenth century, smallpox alone killed off 30% of the indigenous population as they had no immunity against such viruses. The white man forcibly removed the Indians from their accessorial homes as the old and new worlds collided, starting in the east and by the nineteenth century spreading across to the west. Incredibly during the American Revolution some Native Indians fought with the British in the vain hope that colonial defeat would bring a halt to colonial expansion. Some hope! The United States Government did make some efforts to appease the Indians, such as the 1871 Appropriations Act, which gave some Indian Cherokee tribal chiefs US citizenship and recognised the various native nations. However, the most important part was the recognition of tribal sovereignty, independent of the state but not federal law. This was the first true recognition of the Native Indians' rights to co-exist alongside the new settlers.

I found it a little strange that the indigenous Indians lived on reservations and had not integrated more into society, but I had no previous understanding of Indian culture, history or the 1871 Appropriations Act, which of course I had never heard of. I guess initially this suited both parties and maybe still does, but I found it hard to get my head round two parallel societies co-existing in the same space living completely different lifestyles. Here in the desert, New York City may as well be on the moon; it was completely unrelatable. That wasn't to say that non-Indians such as Stevie and me couldn't be here any more than Indians would be excluded from living in the cities, in fact over fifty percent of all Native Indians do live in cities, but often as local communities, but as a rule of thumb there was very little integration.

Hal had also been very proud of the fact the American Indians had fought in both the Civil War – for both the Union and the Confederacy – and the Second World War. He liked to tell anyone he met about this as in his view it was suppressed history. The only thing I did actually know was the 1924 Indian Citizens Act, which gave all Native Indians born in the USA automatic US citizenship. This was led and legislated by our old cowboy friend, President Coolidge. He may have been somewhat unconventional but at least his passion for 'cowboys and Indians' did actually achieve something positive for the Indian tribal communities.

Meanwhile back in Kayenta we were immediately aware we were strangers and white strangers at that. We were nervous about putting the tent up as it was all privately-owned Indian land. It was noticeable there were drunken Indians roaming about and a pack of wild dogs barking in the distance. Indian village or not, in the middle of Kayenta was a Holiday Inn. It did seem an extreme contradiction to have a mainstream hotel in such a place, but I guess the Indians were happy to sacrifice their pride for the mighty dollar; after all, commercialism reigns supreme in the USA and the Navajo Indians were no different to anyone else in that respect. We couldn't afford to stay at the Holiday Inn but made our way to the back of the lobby and lay down on some fairly comfortable sofas. No one paid us any attention or seemed to mind at all. We went to sleep undisturbed for the entire night.

The guy last evening was right. There was hardly any passing traffic and it took us a good couple of hours to thumb a lift out of Kayenta the next morning. A retired couple from Florida in an old 1963 Buick Wildcat gas-guzzler pulled over for us and we said we wanted to see Monument Valley, 'No problem, that's just what we are going do, happy to have you guys along with us.' It was at moments like this I am convinced God in his wisdom is looking out and protecting us. I don't know what Steve felt but I really did feel blessed. The chap introduced himself.

'Langham Harvey and my wife Ariadne, our friends call us Langie and Arrie.' Really, only in America could they have names like this. These two were young seventy-five-year-olds. I suspected they were a little bored with each other's company as it's a long drive from Florida to Utah with no one else to talk to. We certainly broke the mould!

'You've driven all the way from Florida in this car?' I asked.

'Sure have, boy. This ole thing done over a quarter million miles and never let me down yet.' I kept my fingers crossed.

We approached a barrier with a small weathered metal sign which simply read 'Monument Valley' and in small script underneath 'Indian Navajo Reservation'. Beside the barrier was a small rustic-looking wooden hut. It actually looked like a rejected Buckingham Palace sentry box, somewhat faded in the sun. A Navajo Indian with his long black hair tied back, wearing jeans, stepped out and asked Langie for five dollars, 'That is one dollar for each of you and one for the car.' That was it; no retail shop, no car park, no lodging or campsite, no nothing. Just Monument Valley. Langie said, 'If you got Monument Valley on your doorstep I guess you don't need anything else.' I couldn't have put it better myself.

Langie followed the dirt track, which was a forty-mile circular route twisting through and around the valley. Stevie and I had been fortunate over our epic tour to date to have seen some of the most astounding and awe-inspiring landscapes in the world, not least the mighty Grand Canyon, which is almost beyond description. But here in the still and wonder of Monument Valley I felt I was in the most beautiful place in the world. The big screen had certainly drawn me in, but actually to be here and see it with my own eyes was like nothing I had experienced before. The sheer beauty of the place was mesmerising. Langie stopped at various dirt laybys and viewing points. At one viewing point the twentieth century had made its mark where a small story board had been installed explaining the history and geology. Monument Valley is actually a plateau and over hundreds of millions of years the softer sands and rocks had been eroded by the wind and rain leaving these awesome monoliths. Made up of sandstone shale and siltstone, they contained an iron oxide which gave them their red colour. I stood there and could see clearly in my mind John Wayne on his horse, a wagon trail and Indians on horseback. And then suddenly Indians on horseback became a reality; five mounted Indians cantered past within a hundred feet of us. This place was unchanged over many millions of years and even the Red Indians had been here for a few thousand years too.

We must have spent a good four hours hypnotised and spellbound by the magic and rugged charm of Monument Valley before Langie said, 'Well boys we have to get going up to Colorado Springs,' and dropped us off on the Highway 163. We made it up towards Arches National Park and got several good lifts all the way to the old Mormon pioneer town of Moab. Stevie and I just lay down on our sleeping bags by the side of the road and stared at the stars before finally drifting off into a deep sleep.

'Arches' was yet another spectacular natural phenomenon of nature. As the name suggests the rugged landscape has sculptured a series of natural sandstone arches, windows, spire and crossbeams due to long-term erosion and varying weather patterns over millions of years dating back to the Jurassic period. Spectacular towers, sweeping coves, shapes resembling figures of men and animals, balanced rocks and other weird forms resulting from the combined action of running water, wind, rain, frost and sun form a setting to which the arches are a majestic culmination.

We obtained a permit which allowed us to walk around and through these wonders of nature. As ever the sunshine was bright and fierce, the skies were a perfect shade of blue, without a cloud to be seen. Because there was no heavy industry within hundreds of miles of here, pollution didn't exist, making the light intensity remarkably strong and the air pure and clear. Looking through the buff gold arches to the perfect sky was just another dream-type scenario of perfect bliss.

There were few people in the National Park, but we did meet a couple who came and spoke to us. Aleida was Dutch and Hugh came from Ventnor in the Isle of Wight. I don't know why coming from the Isle of Wight should be amusing but it was, and both Steve and I smiled and sniggered a bit. The Dutch girlfriend became quite irate.

'Why is it as soon as Hugh says he comes from the Isle of Wight, all English people start laughing?'

'I really don't know,' I said, 'no reason.'

'It always happens,' she continued defensively. 'It really annoys me and what's worse is you don't know why you find it funny.'

'Well sorry, no offence meant, Hugh,' Stevie chorused, still slightly smirking. Hugh didn't seem to mind and gave us a 'couldn't care less' type shrug.

This still didn't satisfy Aleida, who started to berate Hugh for being too passive. 'You should tell those blokes to not be so bloody rude and not just take it.'

'Look leave it, Aleida, they said sorry. I'm used to it.'

'Arrrgh,' she screamed and stormed off under an arch. Hugh followed meekly behind like a lost puppy dog.

'Christ, talk about neurotic women. Glad she's not my girlfriend,' I whispered to Steve.

'Probably the wrong time of the month,' he drily replied.

After a long day we found a 'dry wash' in which to spend the night. We were a bit concerned as an electrical storm with incredible bolts of lightning passed over, but the rain never came, which was just as well as more likely than not we could have been washed away by a flash flood! Although we were wise to it, we were bloody stupid to risk it.

Sunday 17th September was a long haul on the road, travelling all day to ultimately reach Masa Verdi National Park in Colorado. It took a gutty ten hours and eight separate lifts but we made it by 7.30p.m. We bought bread, cheese and beans, climbed into the tent and had a serious farting session and probably gassed ourselves to sleep! The main attraction of the Masa Verdi is a long sandstone cliff. Approximately halfway up the cliffs are several very large natural caves. Inside these caves the indigenous Indians had built complete villages where whole communities existed for their own protection; they dated back some eight hundred years. They were first re-discovered in 1888 when two local ranchers chanced upon it while searching for stray cattle. 'Spruce Tree House' has an incredible 114 separate rooms or chambers which it was estimated housed over five-hundred people. It measured 216 feet by 89 feet, all housed inside a natural cave. A large spruce tree was found growing from the front of the dwelling to the top of the Messa Verde Cliff. It was thought the men first entered the ruin by climbing down the tree only to discover the lost cave village. Unfortunately the Spruce was cut down by another early explorer. I found it fascinating and of great historic interest.

Walking back down we came across a group of five or

six people listening to a guy playing a guitar. He wasn't really busking, it was more a of a spontaneous sing-song. He launched into Eric Clapton's 'Lay down Sally' from his recent Slowhand album, which he played note perfect and sang perfectly too. Three of the girls were swooning over the guitarist. I had no idea who he was, but it was apparent he was a professional musician and claimed to have worked with Clapton. Who knows?

Later that evening we got a lift in a Winnebago as far as Bayfield. In a great display of double standards, I let my feelings about Winnebago occupants fall to one side as we really appreciated the lift. We found a spot on the side of the road and lay down under the stars in our sleeping bags and just used the tent as a loose cover. Just as well as the next morning it was covered in dew. Having studied the map closely and read quite a few tourist leaflets and US holiday brochures, Stevie and I decided on a visit to Santa Fe in New Mexico as we thought it might be interesting. It wasn't too far from where we were, so we made haste for the oldest state capital in America.

We flagged down a lift with a nice Californian couple called Rupert and Carman. They asked if we minded diverting off the interstate with them to go via 'The Cross'. It sounded like a British pub, but was in fact a small landmark where the four states of Colorado, Arizona, Utah and New Mexico meet. The Cross itself is actually inside Navajo territory, so again was not commercialised. I liked that. A small metal cross on the ground was literally the meeting point of all four States.

I put my left leg in Colorado, my right leg in Utah and leant forward so my right hand was in Arizona and my left hand in New Mexico.

'There you are, guys, I am now in all four states at once.'

Stevie casually walked towards me and instead of asking me to move, stood beside me, his legs apart in Colorado and Arizona and leant right across my back so his hands were in Utah and New Mexico. I collapsed under his weight and the two of us went into a fit of girlish giggles. Our Californian hosts joined in the fun, resulting in a pile of four idiots sprawled to all four parts of the Cross much to the amusement of various onlookers, who suspected we were all drunk.

Rupert and Carman dropped us off in quite a remote spot twenty miles short of Santa Fe where the traffic was flying past at great speed, so it took a while to persuade any car to slow down and pull in for us. Finally after a good couple of hours a very smart and elegant gent, driving an upmarket pickup truck slowed up and gave us a lift. His name was Colonel Ed Sweeney, a former US Airforce pilot who was intriguing. He said originally he arrived in the US as a young boy from Poland with just twenty dollars in his pocket. I didn't delve into the whys and wherefores, but I reasoned Poland in the 1930s was a good place to leave, especially as Herr Hitler was planning a major land grab with devastating consequences. We stopped just outside of town at a soda bar, where admittedly being pressed by me he went into his life history. He served in the US Airforce from 1940–1970 and mentioned he had flown spy planes over the Middle East but was generally evasive and modest. The colonel was equally interested in us, especially Steve hitching such vast distances over two consecutive years. After forty minutes he said, 'If you guys want, you are more than welcome to stay at "the ranch", we have plenty of spare rooms.' As was normal for us our plans were completely fluid and while we had no wish to impose ourselves, Colonel Sweeney was a very persuasive and entertaining man so we readily agreed. His ranch was awesome and seemed to stretch into the distance and beyond the horizon. As for the house; well there were too many rooms to count accurately. His wife Maisey seemed more than a little surprised when we arrived on the doorstep, there was no question we smelt and were in dire need of a good shower. The colonel made the introductions and made it very clear to his petite wife that we were their guests for the night and we were very welcome. It was just that I'm really not sure Maisey agreed!

After we had showered and made ourselves as presentable as possible we sat in their vast plush living room. Above the mantelpiece hung a genuine Japanese samurai sword. I asked him directly if he had acquired it in the Pacific during the war. He just said 'spoils of war' and didn't elaborate. A housemaid brought in a platter of snacks and exotic fruits. Mrs Sweeney made it clear that neither she nor her husband drank alcohol. That was fine with us; our livers needed a rest. He said since retiring from the Airforce he had become a farmer and grew pecans, corn and had a few head of cattle – he didn't say how many but from what we could see, quite a few hundred.

We were introduced to the downstairs pool room and shown our sleeping quarters. Stevie and I felt honoured to have met this man and be invited to his home. Pool was not my game but we played a few frames before the night was through.

In the morning while just generally looking at the walls of the pool room I perused family pictures of the Sweeneys, some with their kids, some with grandchildren, some with military colleagues. I happened across a framed certificate signed by Richard Nixon – it was headed with an embossed American Golden Eagle and NASA space agency logo.

Apollo 11 Moon Landing Mission
Colonel Edward Sweeney
In recognition of your outstanding contribution

Apollo 11 Mission
Space and Moon Landing Project

With thanks and appreciation

Richard M Nixon
President of the United States of America

20th July 1969

'Fuck me,' said Steve, 'who is this guy?' We went upstairs to breakfast and casually mentioned the certificate. The colonel just said 'yes I had a small role' and clammed up. Maisey, overhearing the conversation, put the toast on the table, poured the coffee, stood tall and proud with her hands on her hips and said, 'He headed up the whole Goddamn thing,' and left the room. Colonel Sweeney looked a little abashed and said, 'Not exactly, many people were involved doing all sorts of things,' and left it at that.

Later that morning in a downtown bar in Santa Fe, having thanked Ed and Maisey profusely for their congeniality and generosity, we were discussing the last twenty-four hours and still trying to make sense of what we had seen and heard. Had we really met the guy who headed up the first man landing on the moon mission? Was this guy a war hero in the Japanese campaign? What was his involvement in the Vietnam conflict: spy planes in the Middle East? Wherever the truth lay, there was no question this man was a mover and shaker and without question an achiever. It was all so incredible. I sat there thinking if only those bastards at the Grove Secondary Modern School could see me right now! Whatever the colonel's credentials, he was certainly a decent, generous and fantastic bloke to have met and a real gentleman.

'Downtown' Santa Fe, founded 1607, was a very interesting place. At its heart is a large square Central Plaza where some of the oldest buildings in the United States are situated including St Francis Cathedral, the Palace of Governors and the San Miguel Mission, all built around the early seventeenth century. Santa Fe has a slightly tenuous claim of the oldest House in the USA, the Pueblo of Analco dating from 1200 AD. However, most of the House is built from adobe bricks and corner fireplaces which were only used after the Spanish arrived in 1540. Technically only St Augustine in Florida is older, as Santa Fe was part of Mexico right up to 1847 and therefore not in the USA at that point. The US federation as we know it today was fully established, following the Mexican war where both New Mexico and California were ultimately transferred to the US for a sum of $30m!

The local people were very welcoming and friendly but after four hours we decided to hitch across to Albuquerque, which we were told was only one hour southwest of Santa Fe. We were delighted to hitch just one lift and sure enough an hour later we were in downtown Albuquerque. Sadly after the delights of Santa Fe, Albuquerque was a big let-down; we found it doleful and lugubrious. We made a fairly quick decision to head back west again and made reasonable progress with a Navajo Indian woman car driver who was extremely entertaining and comical to talk to in so much as she was great at poking fun at everything and everyone, including us. She was very interested in our mission to hitchhike around Canada and the USA.

She tried to imitate our accents, which was actually nothing like us. She knew it, we knew it and none of us could stop laughing. She really had it in for Jimmy Carter and actually got his voice fairly well. We'd never met an Indian, male or female who was so different and hilariously funny. Her genes were definitely a bit mixed up; although she put it down to the friends she mixed with in Omaha Nebraska, where she had been to college in her youth. Steve said, 'I passed through Omaha last year on the way to Denver.'

'Gosh you guys get about a bit. I thought you said you arrived in New York in May,' she said.

'True,' agreed Steve, 'I came back again.'

'Not me, I was in Hastings last year,' I chipped in.

'What Hastings, Nebraska?' she seemed alarmed.

'No Hastings, England, where we live,' I explained.

She seemed relieved.

She dropped us at a place called Gallup at 9p.m. and we bought a meal and coffee in an ordinary diner and in time-honoured tradition zonked out in our tent at the side of the road.

10.   The Switchblade Hoodlum, Mr Spock And The Polish Pope

We returned to the ordinary diner for breakfast and to establish the correct time. Much sodding good that was, as the only clock was on Oklahoma time!

Gallup was a slightly desolate place, so it was an easy decision to keep heading west. After two hours, a Latin-looking fella driving a Volkswagen VW Beetle screeched to halt to pick us up. Lopez was chatty and friendly enough, he said he had a bit of Spanish, Mexican and American blood in him. It was also clear he was a bit of a dodgy character, maybe a little bad and definitely liked his cocaine. He said he had been driving half the night and asked me if I would drive while he took a kip on the back seat. I was actually very pleased to drive for a change. It was a real joy to bomb along an American Highway at 80 mph in a dead straight line, without changing gear for 160 miles. Lopez stirred and suggested we pull over to a service area to refuel and buy some grub. Stevie and I headed straight for the gents' toilet or 'restroom' as they call it in these parts. Lopez followed us in and stretched his arms, gave his wrists a flick and a switchblade knife appeared from under his sleeve into each hand. My life flashed in front of my eyes. Oh fuck, I thought, is this bastard going to kill me right here in some non-descript khazi in the middle of nowhere? I saw Stevie take a big stride backwards. Lopez smiled and said, 'These are my protection, no one messes with me, these are made from the finest Spanish steel.' He folded the blades back and had a pee! I was even more convinced Lopez was well on the wrong side of the law; he was one tough son of a bitch who hadn't been intending to terrorise us, but just demonstrate his credentials and immaturity.

Stevie and I looked at each other in some disbelief and agreed he wasn't a threat to us any more than we were a threat to him and climbed back in the car. Lopez was undoubtedly a hoodlum, but for all his faults was bloody funny and handed round burgers and Pepsi at his own expense. In all, Lopez drove us 350 miles in his old clapped-out VW Beetle and dropped us at a 'Dairy Queen' at a town called Kingman in Arizona. We bought a milkshake and a local lady spotting our unusual accents said she could take us a further fifty miles, which we happily accepted. She didn't ask if we were Australian, which was one up to her, but when we told her we were from Great Britain she said, 'Oh isn't that near Italy someplace.' Stevie confirmed it was sort of in that direction! We were dropped off at a turning for Lake Havasu City. It was getting dark and wonderfully warm, so we just sprawled on top of the tent and looked at the stars. We had seen a few lovely night skies here in the States and Canada but tonight was out on its own. The stars were just magical; we could see hundreds if not thousands of them. It was simply the most beautiful sky I had ever seen.

I vaguely remembered as a child the saga of London Bridge being bought by the Americans. Originally built over the River Thames in central London in 1835, it had sadly come to the end of its useful lifespan and was heading for the knackers' yard and set to be replaced and updated by a bridge fit for the twentieth century. However, fate intervened and it was sold to one Robert McCulloch in 1967 for $2.5m and transferred and re-built brick by brick at Lake Havasu City in the Arizona dessert. McCulloch was a fabulously wealthy eccentric business man who, having some years earlier bought a thousand acres at Havasu, had created an embryonic tourist oasis. The acquisition of London Bridge would be his jewel in the crown and really put Lake Havasu City on the map. Arguably McCulloch had bought the world's largest antique! When asked the secret of his success he was quoted as putting it down to 'booze and broads'. In fact he was a very shrewd operator and made his fortune in oil and automobiles.

Now ten years on, McCulloch's tourist oasis was in full swing and Stevie and I were both walking across London Bridge for the second time in our lives, they just happened to be thirteen years and 5500 miles apart! McCulloch had gone to town, or London Town to be more accurate; he had created a British enclave complete with a red London double-decker bus or two and red post boxes. They even had a British pub, unfortunately, it only served Budweisers and Watneys Red Barrel. Well you can't have everything! Suffice to say it was all a little tacky and tasteless, but that's America for you.

Early afternoon we hitchhiked over to Blyth, a journey of about seventy miles. It took over five hours and many small lifts to reach our destination. One of our lifts was in an ancient 1947 Ford pickup. Firstly the exhaust fell off, then the engine blew up! Anyhow it was after dark when we finally found a place to sleep for the night. I wasn't feeling great; probably a case of too much fast food, bad beer and hot sun, so I didn't sleep at all well. It smelt like a manure heap wherever we were and didn't help my stomach. When we woke the next morning, we could see in the perfect daylight, we had in fact been sleeping next to a huge pile of sheep shit all night. No wonder it stank! It was times like this, with no wash facilities, we questioned our sanity.

Blyth it had to be said was the 'arsehole of the world' and we were keen to get out of there. We got a lift to Desert Springs, walked into a very snazzy-looking hotel, kept our heads down and went route one to the bathroom. There was no bath in the bathroom but we stripped down to our Y-fronts and washed the best we could at the sink. A couple of old boys came in for a slash and were more than a bit surprised to see two Limeys covered in soap and water from head to toe. Just across the road from the hotel I spotted a barber and decided that maybe after four months I should have my hair trimmed, as it was starting to look wild. My hair was thick and wavy but never ever grew long and straight, just out and tangled like a bramble bush. While there I was talked into a Turkish-style wet shave with a cut throat. It was actually a very satisfying experience. Stevie, now with quite a full beard, settled for a hair trim only. While I was being shaved, Stevie went back to the hotel and, looking smarter and important and showing some bottle, asked to use the reception phone and called up Guy in Redlands and asked if it was convenient to turn up. We had been planning on going to the Joshua Tree National Park, but Stevie was very keen to head straight on to Redlands, near San Bernardino. There was no question that the Good Lord in his Heaven was looking out for us, as with sheer good fortune yet again we secured a long lift for the best part of four hundred miles in an enormous truck carrying steel coils. Not only were we starting to believe in miracles, we were starting to rely on them. It took most of the day but we knocked on Guy's door just after 6p.m. Guy's partner Herbie answered the door, who instantly recognised Stevie and gave him a big bear hug. There was no question Herbie was quite camp, whereas Guy just didn't give it away at all. 'This is my mate, Richard Wynter,' Steve said and Herbie gave me a big bear hug too!

I was bit confused as Guy had a fantastic pad up in Redwood where he worked at Great American Parkway but shared this house with Herbie down here in Redlands, a good four hundred miles distant. It seems Herbie and Guy had a 50% stake each in Redlands, where Herbie worked as a freelance stage and exhibition designer and Guy owned the Redwood pad outright. Their near neighbours at Redlands were a couple called Debbie and Tim Staningfield, who Stevie had met in the Rockies last year alongside Herbie and Guy, with Marcus Ball. It was Debbie's daughter Rachael who Stevie was lusting over. We were barely though the door before Stevie was on the 'dog & bone' to Rachael. Guy was as generous as previously and with Herbie we all went to a Mexican restaurant for yet more foreign food. Herbie tried to have me believe the restaurant and the food were top notch. Well I thought both were awful, but kept very diplomatic silence as we weren't paying and dare not look Stevie in the eye; I knew exactly what he was thinking. Over dinner Steve said we had been invited down to San Diego to see Rachael and that Debbie would drive us down there tomorrow. We said we would come back up to Redlands in a few days. This seemed to fit better with Guy's plans as he had to go back up to the Bay area for a few days.

Debbie was a very affable lady and treated Stevie as she would a son; he had clearly made more of an impact than I had appreciated last year, maybe more than he'd realised too. Although I got half an impression she thought Stevie had planned all the last four months just to be with Rachael again. He hadn't done that, but there was no question he was very happy to be going to San Diego once again. Debbie drove directly to Rachael's apartment; what neither he, Guy or Debbie had mentioned was she shared it with a girl called Becky who was a vision of beauty. Becky was blonde, busty with a genteel nature and soft voice. She couldn't have been more feminine if she had tried. Both were students at the UCSD (University of California, San Diego). Upon arrival, Debbie insisted the five of us going out for brunch, unfortunately Americanised Mexican again. Unfortunately yet again I thought it was foul!

Debbie returned to Redlands mid-afternoon and left us with the girls. It soon became very clear that the ice hockey boyfriend from last year had fallen through the ice so to speak. Stevie made his move fairly swiftly, which actually surprised me as he is normally very coy and reserved about such things. I suspected a year's pent-up frustration for the two of them meant there was no time to waste. This left me with Little Miss Beautiful; we made plenty of small talk and went for a drive in her old Toyota. By the time we returned, Rachael and Steve were quite open about their sexual liaison, we had a few drinks and I crawled off to sleep on the sofa.

The following day the girls had things to do, so as it was yet another incredibly hot day Steve and I went to the beach. The waves were huge, powerful and relentless; it was quite a workout just concentrating on each one, deciding to dive through them or leap over them. The waves were in a different class to the gentle grey waves of the English Channel. After forty-five minutes of that I was knackered. Sunbathing on the beach Steve enquired, 'Why didn't you sleep with Becky last night?'

'Because she didn't ask me,' I explained.

'Not like you to give it a tug, Rich.'

'Well it is wise to play it carefully – unlike you and Rachael; Christ Stevie, I thought at one point you were going to shag her on the doorstep!'

'Yeah, well it was worth the wait.'

That evening the four of us went to a pub called 'Foggies', which was quite an amazing bar restaurant-cum-nightclub and had quite a bit to drink and the bulk standard burger and fries. Later we got back to the apartment, Rachael and Stevie went straight to the bedroom and Becky played Rod Stewart's Greatest Hits. All was fine until we reached the 'Tonight's the Night' track. I looked at her in the eye and sang along:

'Don't say a word my virgin child
Just let your inhibitions run wild
The secret is about to unfold
Upstairs before the night's too old
Because tonight's the night, it's gonna be alright.'

She blushed turned it off and said, 'You only have to ask, you haven't even kissed me yet.' She made a good point. So I kissed her long and hard and she made love to me soft and gently. I had never been much of a fan of Rod Stewart, but I had a lot to thank him for!

The following day, Monday 25th September, Stevie and I were making our way back down to the beach when unbeknown to us a there was a mid-air collision between an inbound Boeing 727 from LA carrying 125 passengers and seven crew and a small private Cessna light aircraft with two occupants. Everyone was killed, plus a further twenty-two on the ground. The plane came down in the North Park district of the city, probably about three and half miles from where we were at that exact moment, but in flying time, maybe we missed it by about a minute. At the moment of impact we were not at all sure what was happening, but I did see in the distance the airliner coming down even though I hadn't realised it had hit another plane. Stevie and I were focused on taking the right route to the beach and I must have turned away to check something. I didn't hear the crash or explosion, assuming there was one, but couldn't but help see a very large plume of white,

179

grey and black smoke in the distance. Even then I don't think I really registered what I was seeing and didn't fully appreciate the enormity of what had happened until I heard about it on the TV that evening. We had enjoyed another sun-soaked day on the beach while all those poor people had fallen out of the skies and lost their lives. Becky said, 'Just one minute and it could have been you two underneath. Arguably you have just used up one of your nine lives.'

Steve replied with a very sombre face, 'Well yeah, it would have taken out half the downtown area of San Diego and thousands of people with it.' Not something we were likely to forget.

The girls had asked us if we were planning to go down to Mexico; it wasn't something we had really considered, but the more we discussed it the more appealing the idea became. It sounded very different and incredibly cheap. We could travel long distances by train or bus for a couple of dimes. The one obvious concern I had was Mexican food, as I really didn't like it. Rachael made it clear if we went to the larger hotels they would all offer an international menu. I guessed that meant they would sell me a hamburger, not really a great improvement but at least I could stomach them. Becky added there was a Mexican consulate in San Diego and we could get a 'tourist card' there. So we went along and did just that, just in case we decided to venture south.

The four of us had a day out in Tijuana just over the border from San Diego. The only Tijuana I had ever heard of was Herb Albert and the Tijuana Brass with 'This Guy's in Love with You' number one in the UK in 1969 and one of my mother's favourite records. The real Tijuana I found a strange experience, as if the town only seemed to exist to entertain and trade with American tourists. Arguably that was true, but surely this could not be representative of the real Mexico. I got the impression the town had been built and grown up way back in the last century and had not progressed. It felt as though we had stepped back in time. It had a series of plazas or squares all containing markets of various descriptions from soft fabrics to fast foods, leather goods to traditional Mexican clothing. The many Mexicans themselves wore mainly Western-style clothes and generally looked smarter than most of the visitors. Suffice to say I didn't attempt to eat until we returned to 20th-century America.

We spent a few more days making out with the girls and enjoying the beach and the incredible hot temperatures. Unfortunately all good things come to an end, and after four full days Stevie and I returned to Redlands with the promise to meet up and say goodbye to Becky and Rachael at the weekend.

We spent a couple of uneventful days back up at Guy and Herbie's home recharging the batteries. On Friday evening Guy said, 'Right then, guys, we are all going to Disneyland tomorrow the four of us plus Rachael and Becky.' He slapped down six thick books of Disneyland tickets on the kitchen table and said, 'We're all gonna have a good time tomorrow.' It turned out that Guy through his contacts at the Great American Parkway had some sort of reciprocal complimentary ticket arrangement with Disneyland; I guess they are all in the same business and in effect had secured six books of VIP tickets which gave access to absolutely everything.

The girls travelled up by train and we met them at the station at ten o'clock and we all drove to Disneyland. We all had a thoroughly enjoyable day at the world's greatest theme park. I loved the size and complexity of the rides such as Space Mountain, The Matterhorn, Amazon Trip, Pirates of the Caribbean etc. Becky was particularly keen to go to the Mickey Mouse fifth birthday parade. It was a classic American parade with majorettes, with legs up to their armpits, a brass band dressed in white sequin satin jumpsuits with gold trim and the Great Mickey sitting in a sedan chair like a Roman Emperor waving to the raucous crowd, carried by four Mini Mickeys. That evening, much to our embarrassment, Debbie and Tim Staningfield also joined us for a barbeque at Guy's and Herbie's garden. Neither Stevie nor I had any idea if they knew what we had been up to with their daughter and friend, but if they did they didn't show any resentment or hostility whatsoever, indeed quite the opposite. Maybe they were more liberal than we gave them credit for; the only downside was the girls slept over at Debbie and Tim's and not with us. Stevie came up with one of his dry quips, 'Probably Herbie wouldn't approve of straight sex in his house!'

On Sunday morning the girls and us all went back down by train to San Diego. Rachael had secured four tickets to see the San Diego Padres v Los Angeles

Dodgers. After my experience of baseball in Toronto I was a little sceptical, but I was very happy to be with Becky so went along. There was a great atmosphere and someone called Gaylord Perry who, being hyped as a Baseball God, made his 300th career strike out in this match, I assumed that meant wicket and the crowd went mad. Comparisons with cricket were pointless so I enjoyed the spectacle, ate popcorn and drank root beer – not to be recommended, it tasted like Mackeson without the alcohol – and cheered along with everyone else. We all returned back for our final night with the girls, happy especially as the Padres had won 4–3. We all knew we were highly unlikely to ever meet again and for the second time in just over six weeks it was very hard to say goodbye to a woman who would have been all too easy to fall in love with under more normal circumstances. But both Stevie and I felt we were on a crusade to complete our mission of hitchhiking right around North America and mustn't be steered or seduced from our course; in that respect we were very single and bloody-minded. First thing Monday morning we hitched back up to Redlands.

Way, way back in 1910 my great grandmother died of tuberculosis. Two years later my great grandfather and his five children immigrated to Long Beach California. However, after just eighteen months Margery Grace Carlton aged just fourteen, my future grandmother, suffering from terrible home sickness, decided to return home to Bristol into the guardianship of a vicar, one Homer Green, some thirty years her senior, who would ultimately become my grandfather. She left behind in the US her father, three sisters and a brother, none of whom she would ever see again. Two of those three sisters, Dolly and Dotty had passed away. My grandmother died in 1945 aged just forty-six of cancer, a full decade before I was born. Grandad Green died just six months after I was born. This left Great Aunt Nettie and Great Uncle Bob, both of whom still lived in Longbeach, California sixty-six years on. They were old; Bob was eighty-one and Nettie eighty-five.

Guy or Herbie had requisitioned a nearby neighbour to drive us to Long Beach, which was seventy-five miles due west of Redlands. It was good of neighbour Thelma to take us, but she just didn't stop rabbiting the whole way about the state of the economy, the state of some American football team I had never heard of, her lazy good-for-nothing son, the LA traffic, the LA smog, the dope-pushers and God knows what else. It was a monologue of moans and we couldn't get a word in edgeways even if we had wanted to. After an hour-and-a-half I couldn't get out of her car quickly enough.

I had spoken with Barbara Kaste and Great Uncle Bob (Carlton) by phone the day before and now here we were in Bob's pleasant bungalow in a Long Beach suburb. Barbara was Bob's daughter and Brett his idiot grandson. Bob just could not have been more American; he had a strong West Coast accent, wore a classically loud shirt and sported a big bushy silver moustache. Bob introduced us to his second wife, Middie; she was equally as delightful and welcoming.

Bob was so pleased to meet me and made Stevie feel equally at home; they were so easy to talk to and much younger at heart, which belied their years. He told me a little about their move from Gloucestershire to the States just before the Great War, and just repeated that his sister Margery could never settle in California and hated the long warm summers. Interestingly he also mentioned unsolicited that they had come over a couple of weeks before the *Titanic* went down, 'There by the Grace of God go I,' uttered Bob with a glazed-over expression. Amen to that.

Inevitably he broke out a few ice-cold beers and the conversation, banter and great wit carried on well beyond midnight. At about 1a.m. Middie said to Bob, 'Now come on "Tiger", it is time for bed!' The mind boggled.

Bob and Middie absolutely insisted we could stay just as long as we liked and to use their home as a base, but today (Thursday 5th October) Bob drove just me to see his one surviving sister Nettie who lived in a sheltered care home a few miles away. Unlike Bob, Nettie had retained her English accent and in some ways her English mannerisms and way of life. Most of all she was a dead image of my own mother, or how she would most likely look in another thirty years' time. She struggled to get up from her chair, shook my hand and said, 'Oh you wear those do you?' It seemed Great Aunt Nettie had a life-time aversion to denim jeans. I was extremely proud of my Levi's; I apologised for my appearance and told her apart from a pair of shorts and swimming trunks, I had nothing else with me.

Nettie and her two now deceased sisters, always known to my sisters and me as the 'American Aunts', were all spinsters. When we had been children they had always sent us Christmas cards and on our birthdays had always sent a card and three one-dollar bills, one each I guess. Nettie showed pictures of the three sisters on holiday in England around about 1960 and there was a very youthful looking Mum and Dad and me aged four, Rose aged six and baby Cathy a few months old. I didn't remember this at all. As pleased as I was to have finally met one of my American Aunts, I was saddened at how distant and bitter she had become. If I had met Bob and her in the street I would never in a million years have known they were brother and sister. She was in essence still very British, while he was American through and through. Great Aunt Nettie was demure, introverted and cold; Great Uncle Bob was big, brash and humorous. The three of us went out to lunch, which to be fair Nettie insisted on paying for. I knew she kept in reasonably close contact with my mother, but I found the conversation stifled and awkward. I somehow felt I didn't quite meet her expectations of me. After a couple of hours Bob and I departed, but I promised to come to say goodbye to her before we moved on next week. We picked up Stevie and made our way down to the docks at Long Beach where the big attraction was the decommissioned P&O *Queen Mary* cruise liner, which permanently berthed there. We were both particularly keen to visit the *Queen Mary* to see if the St Leonards Marina building was as accurate as we had been led to believe.

I don't know what the new owners of the *Queen Mary* were thinking of, but I thought it was appalling as they had completely commercialised the ship. The main sun decks were full of things like the 'frozen banana stand', burger stands, popcorn, gift shops and a vulgar shop selling *Queen Mary* replica crew uniforms. I was disappointed and quickly lost interest in it and dreaded to think what Great Aunt Nettie would have said about this!

Over the next few days Stevie and I travelled a lot by local buses to places like the downtown area of LA, Pasadena, Santa Monica and pier, Beverley Hills, Hollywood Boulevard and Sunset Strip. These were all of course well known to us as they feature in such a high proportion of TV series and movies. We had no desire to 'take the tour' or clamber aboard an open-top double-decker bus and gawk at the movie stars' villas. We gawked for free by walking miles and miles in the unrelenting heat. Sunset Strip had a little of the San Francisco feel about it with an interesting selection of characters and odd-bods. Most people were polite and friendly but I felt their ulterior motive more often than not was to sell you something or other I almost certainly did not want, need or afford.

Bob and Middie were sold on a place called Knotts Berry Farm. It sounded like one of those new pick-your-own-fruit places we had springing up back home, but turned out to be yet another theme park. We went at Mid's insistence but sadly after the Great American Parkway, Magic Mountain and Disneyland this was a poor distant relation. On the Sunday,

Middie asked if we wanted to come to church with them. Out of respect for family and God (probably in that order) I decided I would, although I knew Stevie would decline. Nettie met us at the church. Because my mother was a vicar's daughter I was used to quite low Church of England services. This church was more Anglican Catholic, so I was really surprised by high mass and communion. I was only surprised in the sense I had just assumed they, being Mum's aunt and uncle, it would have been similar to the service at home. Dad on the other hand would have loved it.

Way back in early July we stumbled across a guy called Barry Barrie at a hotel at Yellowstone National Park. I recalled he had been a bit creepy and odd, but we had been drinking whiskey with him and Maurice. We had his studio card with his number on and decided to give him a call.

'Yep,' he said. 'The *Star Trek* movie is now in full production and filming is taking place at the Paramount Studios right now. Get yourselves over here tomorrow; I will leave you entry passes at reception.' Glad we called!

So on Monday we made our way to Hollywood and introduced ourselves at the Paramount Studios reception and asked for tickets left by Mr Barrie. 'Oh him,' the surly girl said and virtually threw an envelope at us. We found Studio Four and sure enough inside it was a hive of activity with space junkies, extra-terrestrials, Enterprise crew members plus an assortment of stage hands, lighting crew and cameramen everywhere. It all seemed a bit chaotic. We asked at least ten people if they knew where we could find Barry Barrie; most feigned complete indifference but eventually someone pointed and said 'that's him over there'. We strode over and said 'Hi.'

'Great to see you guys, just do your own thing and enjoy the day. I'll catch you later,' and with that he was gone as though he had been beamed up. Barrie looked harassed and pressurised and a little nervous; Hollywood wanted their pound of flesh out of their guys. We thought, alright then, let's just stroll about, just like the man said. We bumped into a beautiful Hollywood starlet in a tight blue blouse and slacks, holding a clipboard.

'Hi are you guys with the Trekkie Tour?'

As quick as flash Stevie responded, 'No we're with the Woolwich.' She looked dumbfounded and turned on her heel and marched away in a huff. We turned the other way and nearly bumped into William Shatner and DeForest Kelly (Captain Kirk and Doctor McCoy) walking on to the set wearing their swanky new uniforms. Neither looked very pleased to see us, Shatner half nodded while Kelly fixed us with a very hard, threatening stare; the last time a person looked at me like that they kicked the shit out of me at the Grove School! Stevie was both irritated and amused by Kelly's lack of grace and started to chuckle quietly to himself.

They were shooting a scene in the SS Enterprise hospital theatre room. The six beds looked like a series of ironing boards protruding from the wall at right angles in the shape of a horseshoe.

Mr Spock (Leonard Nimoy) was signing autographs

for a gang of star-struck *Star Trek* fans and they weren't even the Trekkies official tour group. I wondered if he signed them Leonard Nimoy or Mr Spock! At one point a stage hand told us to 'get out of here', I wasn't sure if he meant by a few feet or out of Paramount Studios. We stayed and got in someone else's way.

Stevie had always been amused by Scotty, the chief engineer and his dreadful faux-Scottish accent, and with great delight Mr Scott (James Doohan) was ushered on to the set. At the sight of Mr Scott, Stevie started to chuckle again in anticipation of some awful dialogue. Sadly we didn't hear any as he was deep in conversation with a producer or editor or whoever he was.

Another all-smiling girl in a tight-fitting blue blouse and slacks, with a security pass, a ring folder and looking very important, asked who we were exactly; we told her we were guests of Barry Barrie. She seemed unsure who he was until Stevie pointed him out across the studio floor holding a large boom. Her smile disappeared 'Oh him,' she said and cringed. 'Well careful where you go, you should only really be here with an official tour group.'

Meanwhile to our great amusement, a woman with a trolley of coffee, soft drinks and snacks wandered through the bridge of the SS Enterprise as though she was on the factory floor. All she really needed was a tea urn, curlers and a rollup hanging out of her mouth to complete the image. It seemed like a classic Monty Python moment; anyhow we took advantage and grabbed a Coca-Cola and finger sandwich. An eminent, serious-looking bloke with big thick sideboards gave us a filthy look. Apparently these were meant for the actors, we sincerely hoped we had eaten Doctor McCoy's rations. Barry reappeared and, pointing to the important looking bloke, said 'that there is Mr Gene Roddenberry himself.' We told him he had given us a filthy look and what the important girl with the smile and the ring folder had said. He explained the passes had been obtained from one of the Paramount Studio senior management and not the *Star Trek* production team, which had effectively bypassed the system, which was definitely frowned upon and partially explained Barry's nervousness. It also sort-of explained why everyone was giving us strange looks and we'd got under too many people's feet, not least 'Bones' McCoy.

We had now seen all we wanted to see and had got the general idea, had generally got in the way and felt we had maybe outstayed our welcome, so we thanked Barry and escaped back to the sanity of Long Beach. We vowed to see *Star Trek – the Motion Picture* at the Classic Cinema Hastings, when it hit the big screens next year.

October 10th was my twenty-second birthday and was the only date I had especially earmarked to be somewhere specific. That somewhere was with Great Uncle Bob & Middie. Unbeknown to me they had been busy organising all sorts of surprises for me. The first of these was an incoming phone call from Mum to wish me many happy returns. Dad came on the line and suggested I returned home and took a job with the Gas Board! I told him not just yet as we were three thousand miles from New York. God, I thought, the bloody Gas Board, no thanks, and promptly forgot all about it.

Bob produced a pile of post including several cards and letters from home. Mum had sent me fifty quid and Dad had sent me a copy of the October *'Cricketer'* magazine, which I couldn't put down. It contained a full report on Sussex's Gillette Cup Victory over Somerset. At 1.00p.m. Great Aunt Nettie arrived by taxi and Bob drove us all to a restaurant on the seafront. I told them that Stevie and I had now gone virtually three weeks without a tin of Dinty Moore Stew, which seemed to amuse old Aunt Nettie very much. It was really the first and only time I saw her laugh.

The big news story of the week following the death of Pope John Paul after just thirty-four days in office, was that the Vatican had elected a Polish Bishop to become Pope, John Paul II. This caused some quite factious and entertaining comments from Bob, Middie and Nettie, who as Anglian Catholics had definite views on Papal succession. All three seemed incredulous that a 'Polack' had been nominated and elected by the pontiffs. To White America, Poles seemed to be held in contempt, they were maligned and ridiculed as if they were from outer space. Americans looked at them the same way the English looked at the Irish, or the Aussies treated New Zealanders. But in the case of America it just seemed a bit harsher and less humorous. However, the best of the comments came from Middie when she said,

'They'll be making Bob Hope Pope next!'

Stevie and I sat back in quiet amusement as the debate raged on the merits of a Polish Pope. Personally it really didn't make any difference to me who was Pope, providing he was up to the job, but Middie and Nettie particularly were very disparaging about the poor chap. Although they sounded jocular, they were quite serious in their views. For them this was a sincere and deliberate discussion. Dave Allen would have loved it!

On our final day in LA we went to Olvera Street, reputedly the oldest and original street in Los Angeles, where we climbed to the top of the court house. We had had spectacular panoramic views of LA despite the smog and spent a couple of hours in the city library on Los Angeles Street, just down from the Dodger Stadium. I liked visiting the libraries, in part to catch up with the news back home as the larger libraries carried copies of UK newspapers, mainly a week or so out of date. *The Times*, *Telegraph* and *Express* were the most prominent. Jimmy the Greek would have been pleased to know there were no 'Red Tops' here in LA library. Sad to discover Brighton and Hove Albion lost again.

The library also offered a range of newspaper publications from across the States. Politics and gun crime dominated the US headlines. Stevie got hold of a copy of the *Wall Street Journal* and was amazed to read that Marvin Gaye had been declared bankrupt.

'How does a guy that hasn't been out of the charts for a decade go bust?' he reasonably asked. 'He must have made an absolute fortune. It says here he's got declared debts of seven million dollars. Try living on $3 a day mate!'

'By the sound of it he soon will be,' I suggested.

Murders and muggings generally were a common daily occurrence and people tended to be immune to the everyday horrors of stabbings, shootings and violence carried out throughout USA on an industrial scale. Some of the stories were incredible. For example on 28th June five people were shot dead in an Irish-themed bar in Boston, Massachusetts according to the *Boston Herald*, believed to be drugs related. Four of the victims were believed to be Irish American gangsters and the fifth, one Jack Kelly, a local Boston TV news anchor. Police were trying to establish if there was a connection between Kelly and the four hoods, no one knows. To date the murders remain unresolved.

A few days before, the *Augusta Daily Gazette* reported the murder of two unidentified people at a truck stop in Missouri. Both had been shot and mutilated and their bodies dumped on the side of the road several miles apart. Again, no one as yet had been apprehended for the murders.

The *Columbus Dispatch* reports in Cincinnati a man was shot to death sitting in his car at a traffic light intersection. Motive unknown. No arrest.

In September the *Los Angeles Times* reported a major 'fire-fight' where two heavily-armed bank robbers were shot dead at the scene of the crime by the LAPD. Seven cops and four civilians caught up in the mayhem received gun wounds. All are expected to survive.

Also last week a woman was shot dead in an LA suburb, possibly gang-related and two others injured. Assassin unknown.

Then there is this guy Ted Bundy, a real nasty piece of work, reported right across the country who is a sadistic serial killer of the worse kind. He is known to have raped and murdered at least thirty women across the US, by strangulation, going back to 1974. He then decapitated the heads and kept them as mementoes in his apartment. Thank God he has been caught at last. One can only hope this guy is given the electric chair.

According to the LA County Sherriff Department a teenage Hispanic male was shot dead after running away, having been stopped for a traffic violation, The *East LA Tribune* reports. The unnamed victim was pronounced dead on arrival at hospital.

The *New York Times* reported that someone walked up to two deputies outside a Bronx subway station and shot them at point-blank range in the back of the head. No reason or motive has been established and the gunman is still at large.

The *Jacksonville Daily Record* reported a local homeless woman was found in a doorway in Jacksonville, apparently shot as she slept. Completely pointless, senseless and without pity. Suffice to say the police are clueless as again, no motive has been established, if indeed there ever was one.

Police in Dallas Texas are looking for a person who shot a middle-aged man in the back while watching his children play at a recreation park. In the same paper, *The Dallas Morning News*, it is reported a twelve-year-old child brandishing a semi-automatic gun was arrested after shooting randomly in the car park of a shopping mall. In this instance only a few flesh wounds were reported. How on earth does a child this age get hold of a gun like that?

Then just yesterday a woman, Nancy Stungen, was stabbed to death in a New York hotel. Her boyfriend, the despicable Sid Vicious of the Sex Pistols punk band, was arrested within hours. Both were high on heroin. She had a reputation for antisocial behaviour and was known to the media as a Nauseating Nancy. Maybe she was, but you wouldn't wish her life to end like this.

The oldest newspaper publication in the USA is the *New Hampshire Gazette*, I found a two month out-of-date copy and the headline was about a mother and teenage son who were gunned down in a food store in Concord, in yet another drugs-related gangland murder. Apparently it was a case of mistaken identity; well that's all right then! It was reported on page four and I got the impression, as sad as it was, no one really seemed to care.

Murder in America may well be a capital offence,

but people are shot dead virtually every day and the gun laws remain unchanged. They can shoot dead the President, John F Kennedy and gun laws remain unchanged. They can shoot dead high profile Senators, such as Bobby Kennedy and the gun laws remain unchanged. They can shoot dead decent principled civil rights leaders such as Martin Luther King and the guns laws remain unchanged. It strikes me any one can shoot anybody and yet the good citizens of the United States just don't seem to get it. Guns kill.

So what is it about Americans and firearms? I find it astounding that Americans cannot divorce their 'right to keep and bear arms' from the highest domestic murder rate in the world. It just defies belief. How can you not associate one with the other? The solution of course is staring them directly in the face: change the fucking constitution and delete the Second Amendment. Problem sorted!

It will never happen, of course, because the powerful 'National Rifle Association' has among its enormous membership many senators and congressmen which, by definition, means it is corrupted and politicised and will always argue in favour of upholding 'constitutional rights'. So as always, the victims' rights die with them, as the US constitution only deals with the living. Another part of the problem is the US Constitution has become a National Institution in its own right and for that reason alone will never change. Another American 'National Institution' is the 'Pledge of Allegiance' to the US flag, which is drilled into every American child from the age of five when kids start out at school.

The Pledge is recited daily in schools across the country, court rooms and military bases and in congressional chambers and numerous other bodies. It is read out loud with the right hand on the left shoulder with the arm across the heart. All very patriotic. It reads:

'I pledge allegiance to the flag of the United States of America and to the republic for which it stands, one nation under God, with liberty and justice for all.' Oh yeah, really? Where was the liberty and justice for the Kennedys and Martin Luther King.

But there you have it the 'Pledge of Allegiance' is very effective brainwashing and the people really buy into it and quote it at every opportunity to bear arms, as justification to keep the second amendment and as justification for their actions, however legal or illegal they may be.

It isn't my problem, but you would think the American people would have more sense and want do something about it. To be fair, with maybe one or two exceptions, just about every American I have met over here seems perfectly normal, rational, balanced and extremely generous and friendly toward to me and Stevie, which makes the whole compliance and unquestioned acceptance of the Second Amendment all the more startling.

God Bless America!

Late afternoon we headed straight for the beach at Long Beach for a good long swim and in the evening we took Bob and Middie out for a pizza for a farewell dinner. It was absolutely my treat and I promised to stay in touch.

11.   Pervert, Quads & Bats; Wish You Were Here?

For the next leg of our adventure we decided to head in the general direction of Phoenix. We spent two really gutty days struggling for lifts and to make any serious mileage standing in the desert in blistering heat, quite possibly about 110F in the shade. At Palm Springs we went to a restaurant called Sambo's; I was surprised it hadn't been burnt to the ground. Maybe the word Sambo didn't have the same connotation over here. On Friday 13th, having been fried alive in the burning sun of the Colorado desert, we found ourselves at an inland lake known as the Salton Sea. There was a two-bit bar called the Salton (not very original) near the railway line, where we had a few beers and crashed out just over the road for the night in the tent. I don't know why we put the tent up as it was so hot. I was woken early in the morning by the heat and when a mile-long goods train rattled slowly past; the noise was incredible. The bar had opened at 6a.m. so we went back in to buy breakfast, which was surprisingly good. The waiter-cum-barman recognised us from the night before and said, 'Was that you over there in the tent?' We said it was us.

'At least there weren't any earth tremors last night.'

'How do you mean?' I enquired.

'Well, we're right on the San Andreas fault right here: get 'em all the time. The lake there is in a depression caused by the shifting tectonic plates.'

He returned to his kitchen and to our amazement

we were chatted up by two birds, Ashley and Frances, who were eating a breakfast of pancakes and syrup, who had heard our British accents.

'Are you guys Australian?'

'Could be,' said Stevie.

They didn't appear confused or bothered by Stevie's non-committal answer and said they and their boyfriends were staying in their campervans a mile down the road and were planning on a day lazing in the sun and drinking beer: 'Why don't you come and hang out?' they asked. Don't ask twice, babe! We were on our way.

They were camped up near the lakeside under a cluster of knackered looking old palm trees. Between the five of them they had two campervans, a pickup truck and three quad trikes. They had the whole area completely to themselves. These guys were what are generally regarded as 'rich college kids', with too much time and money to know what to do with. We could help them out! They actually were very welcoming and open and were very clearly here for a good time. 'Come and join us, we're having a party,' said one of them. One of the campervans was packed with booze, like a small drinks warehouse. They had a fifteen-gallon keg of Budweiser and at least fifty bottles of Coors and Pabst Blue Ribbon, various liquor bottles and a dozen cartons of orange juice. There were three large cool boxes full of all sorts of food.

Steve said, 'Look we should make a contribution towards this if we are going to spend the day here.'

Frances said firmly, 'Absolutely not, I invited you

here as our guests, just help yourself. If we run low we can always buy some more.'

One of the guys said he had to go in to Indio for supplies; I couldn't think for the life of me what else he could possibly want. An hour later he returned with an enormous ice block in the back of the pickup. It was so big it was a wonder it hadn't broken the rear axle.

The guys, Zane, Ryan and Everitt, dug a large pit into the contour of the land, backed up the pickup and pushed, pulled and slid the ice block into the hole. They then used their shovels to break up the ice as best they could. We then lifted the beer keg into it and surrounded the keg with bottles of Coors and Pabst Blue Ribbon and the cartons of orange juice. We were ready to party.

Zane produced a large speaker which he somehow linked up with his vehicle radio cassette system and took Steve and me round to the side of a campervan and said, 'Is there anything in there you particularly like?' We riffled through a large box of cassettes. I had to hand it to these guys they had great musical taste. They had so much good stuff; Zane pulled out Deep Purple 'In Rock'. Stevie said, 'Hey man, we have been to Mount Rushmore.' He'd never heard of it or knew what we were talking about. A lot the cassettes were of newish stuff I wasn't over familiar with, but was very happy to listen to, such as 'Hotel California' by the Eagles (I'd only previously heard the title track). They had a cassette of 'Rumours' by the new Fleetwood Mac. I was biased as since Peter Green's demise I had steered clear of Fleetwood Mac as they gradually lost their way. I'd heard they had a few new female members in the band, but this album was fucking fantastic. Lindsey Buckingham's guitar work was astoundingly good and the girls' harmonies just blended perfectly. Elton John's 'Goodbye Yellow Brick Road', which I had never listened to in its entirety, was a masterpiece.

The guys were well into Todd Rundgen, Steely Dan, Eric Clapton (inevitably: after all he was God), a guy called Bruce Springsteen who had so much energy he was terrific – and Dylan, of course. I was pleased they hadn't bought into the new wave Punk Rock scene, which I don't think was as popular in the States as it was back home. I hated the bloody Sex Pistols – and now even more so after that arsehole Sid Vicious murdered his girlfriend last week – and groups like that; it was predominantly crap, although I thought a couple of groups like the Stranglers and Boomtown Rats had a bit going for them as they seemed more like proper musicians.

The rock music blasted out and the ice-cold beers went down a treat. Everitt powered up his quad trike and set off followed by Ashley and Ryan. These quad trikes were monster machines with 125cc engines, three enormous tyres which looked like they had been lifted from a tractor and were great for speeding over virtually any terrain. Half an hour later they came back and said, 'Do you guys want to give it a go?' It was great fun hurtling across the desert, over mounds, through dry river beds and circling around the dead-looking palm trees and boulders. Mid-afternoon they fired up the barbeque and threw on enormous juicy steaks, chicken legs and corn cobs. The girls worked hard on preparing a variety of salads and potatoes.

We had drunk quite a few beers and eaten exceptionally well. Two of the guys and Ashley were high on dope. They had been incredibly generous and decent towards us and made me feel quite obsequious and respectful. I was feeling drowsy as the sun was becoming lower in the sky. Zane played the Pink Floyd album 'Wish You Were Here'. Again I had never heard this before; as I had taken the view after 'Dark Side of the Moon' they couldn't possibly ever improve on it. I couldn't have been more wrong. I just lay there propped up against a palm tree under the shade, with a cold beer in hand, immersing myself in the incredible music and rugged landscape as the sun changed the colours of the desert sand. The music completely fitted the mood, like a soundtrack – I added it to my list of albums to buy when I got back home.

Stevie and I did our normal thing and laid the tent flat on the ground and slept under the stars. At seven the next morning we walked back down to the Salton for breakfast and a good wash and clean-up. We returned back to the guys to collect our gear and say our farewells. Steve made me laugh when he went right up to Frances and gave her a bloomin' great kiss full on the mouth in front of her boyfriend Ryan.

'Get your tongue out of my mouth, I am trying to say goodbye,' screamed Stevie.

Frances laughed and turned to Ryan, I said, 'No tongues.' Steve just smiled and said, 'Just so you know, we are Brits not Aussies.' I added, 'If we had been Aussies, he would have shagged her too.' All seven of us had a good laugh. We all shook hands and embraced, thanked them one last time and headed on to Phoenix.

It took half the day to get down to El Centro and then we got a lift for well over two-hundred miles to a place called Buckeye, just west of Phoenix, with a real redneck character who was straight out of the 'shoot first ask questions later' camp. He seemed to hate everyone, not least the 'wet-backs' and was anti-everything, except guns of course. He was quite funny in his descriptions of people and situations, but I suspected he didn't have many friends.

We arrived in downtown Phoenix at ten the next morning, dropped our gear off at the Greyhound 'left luggage' hall and found a quite excellent hamburger joint called Wendy's. Having spent a few hours looking about the city I was wondering why I was so keen to visit this place as there was nothing outstanding here. A bit out of habit we identified the tallest city building and decided to take the lift to the top to take in the views. The elevator doors opened and we entered a large conference room full of middle-aged men in sharp business suits drinking glasses of wine. It looked like for all the world to be some boring business convention. However there was something about them that made them all look a bit suspicious. I don't know if it was the New York accents, the cut of their snappy suits or the fact they all looked a bit Italian, or even the lack of normal conference facilities, but I was convinced we'd walked into a Mafia meeting. A hefty-looking bloke, a bit like a classic Mafia boss, came over and demanded to know who we were and what we were doing there. Stevie showed him his camera and said 'just want to some pictures of Phoenix'. He wanted to confiscate the camera which we flatly refused to hand over. With this he summoned a uniformed security officer who escorted us back down the lift and out of the building. Stevie was convinced we had just stumbled into a Mafia convention, masquerading as a business conference. We weren't going to go back to ask, but it was an unnerving fifteen minutes. It could have been; we would never know. Either way we were definitely unwelcome so we collected the backpacks and decided to give Tucson a go.

It was 7p.m. and a slightly odd fella stopped to give us a ride in an old station wagon and asked us both to sit in the back seat; we'd never been asked to do that before. He was a bit quiet and fidgety and came across as a little tense. After ten miles he said, 'If you guys are gay, I know a place we can play about a bit.'

'Look I think you got us wrong, pal,' I said. He turned round to look at us with a horrible leer and I caught sight of a revolver. The gun was on the passenger seat and while the driver had both hands firmly on the steering wheel, I really was extremely concerned about a fucking hand gun being thrown into what was fast becoming a volatile mix.

'Why don't you drop us off right here and now,' I demanded in no uncertain terms. Thank God he did. He dropped us on some dark nondescript corner and sped away. For the first time since we landed at JFK in May I found myself shaking with fear. Steve was as white as a sheet, 'Fucking bastard,' he muttered. 'He could have just as easily as shot us then and we would have been history.'

He was right. All of a sudden I felt very vulnerable. After all the horror stories we heard about and read in the Los Angeles City Library this really did put the fear of God right up us. Two minutes later the pervert's station wagon headed back towards us with his lights out. We tried to blend into a hedgerow; the car kept going, back towards Phoenix.

We didn't know where we were exactly, it was dark and had nowhere to go, so we walked half a mile or so until we came across a bit of scrubland and with some reluctance pitched the tent out of sight of the road.

The next morning feeling a bit fatigued, hungry, hot and sweaty we flagged down what looked like an old school yellow bus, which had been converted into a mobile holiday home driven by a decent couple who said they were going to see the Sonora Desert Museum at Tucson. We clambered in and said we would be happy to go there too. It felt like things were back to normal. We tried to dismiss yesterday as our one and only bad day in nearly five months.

The Sonora was a Natural History Museum which cultivated the flora and fauna, and wildlife of the Arizona desert. The real centrepieces, which were everywhere in the Sonora Desert was the Saguaro cactus tree which can grow up to forty feet high and live two hundred years. These cacti feature on just about every Western movie ever made and in the films are often linked with Monument Valley, which in actual fact is well over four hundred miles north of here. We enjoyed the day here but felt it was too late and the traffic too light to hitch in to Tucson. We decided to stay put, close by the museum, and spent a fairly boring evening in the desert. We didn't even have a tin of Dinty Moore Stew to sustain us, just a melted Hershey bar and a pack of Uncle Joe's mints.

We agreed our priority this morning was food and a shower. Diners and coffee bars in Tucson were easy to find, a shower was not. We eventually came across a women's only YMCA, sold them a good sob story and bunged the girl a couple of bucks to use the shower rooms – it was midday and there was no one about. Tucson was about as quiet as Bexhill-on-Sea; not a comparison often made, as I pointed out to Stevie. We did our best to escape, but sympathetic drivers were in short supply, so after three hours we gave up and found a brilliant diner where I had the largest burger I had ever eaten. We hiked a few miles east out of town and found a parched park in which to settle for the night.

The drivers this morning were no more empathetic or responsive than last evening, so after a couple of hours we hopped on a local bus and travelled five miles and gave it another go on the roadside. Half an hour on, we were sitting in the back of a pickup and went all the way to Las Cruces, New Mexico. For the first time since Bodie we felt cold. The fact we were four thousand feet above sea level may have had something to do with it. We learnt the Las Cruces area was once all Apache country until a mixture of the Spanish invaders and the white

208

settlers virtually wiped them out over two or three centuries. Certainly not something to be proud of.

Foolishly we spent the night under the stars and not under the tent and woke to find our sleeping bags soaked with dew. Our clothes and belongings were damp. We stepped back to the road and were delighted when a black guy pulled over for us within a couple of minutes. Easton was a slightly wild but interesting man who had lived a varied life, and from humble beginnings had become a successful business man, quite in what industry I wasn't sure. We were speeding along talking and minding our own business when he got pulled over by a traffic cop. He was told he was twelve miles per hour over the speed limit and he would have to pay a $50 fine. As if that wasn't bad enough for him he was then directed by the cop to go and see the judge 'right now' and hand the fine over. We followed the cop car to a rundown farmhouse where the judge lived (or so we were told) and Easton paid up. I had no idea if this was a scam or not but it all seemed very odd to me. Easton just shrugged and although obviously not happy, just took it in his stride.

"It happens sometimes. No point in dwelling on it; life's too short."

Easton was a hell of a cool dude. He was inspirational in his understanding and tolerance. I had the utmost respect for him.

We drove via El Paso heading east and Easton said he lived up some remote mountain road and dropped us close to a place called Carlsbad. He suggested if we had time then we should visit the

'Cavern'. We had all the time in the world but not this evening as time was ticking on and sun was starting to go down. We found a fairly remote spot, not far from the Carlsbad Cavern entrance to pitch the tent and witnessed the most extraordinary spectacle when thousands of bats flew out of the cavern. As darkness descended we became aware of how threatening the general area was from mountain lions, bobcats, mule deer, scorpions and rattlesnakes. The vampire bats were the least of our problem!

The next morning we bought a sizable breakfast outside the cavern and paid just a dollar each to visit the caves. Inside there was a signposted three-mile route, which took us four-and-a-half hours to complete as the internal rock formations were quite breathtaking. The lighting was very well managed and angled to show off the many interesting rock and water features. The cavern system itself consisted of over a hundred caves and had evolved over many millions of years by rainwater eroding the soft limestone to leave vast caverns; the perfect home to the many species of bat that live here. Again I found it pathetic that so many of the tourists were more interested in walking through as fast as they could to get to the underground lunch room, as if that was the main attraction. Well I guess for them it was.

That afternoon we hitched a lift to a place called White City with a middle-aged couple from Canada. They seemed to be impressed we were (apparently) so knowledgeable about their country. They said they had met some Texans who didn't seem to know where Canada was! Stevie said we had met some guy who thought the UK was near Italy. Well that's life. Matt and Olivia, our new Canadian friends, said they were heading for a campsite at White City and said we could share their pitch. We readily agreed and were even more pleased to find on site a laundromat and decent shower unit.

12. The Chihuahua Cowshead, Bulls And La Vaselina

Sunday 22nd October – Matt drove us back down to El Paso and left us at a 'Taco Bell', a pseudo-Mexican Restaurant on the outskirts of town. We spent a few hours killing time there as it was starting to rain quite heavily. The restaurant was a bit dead with a few customers on a filthy wet day. I went to the 'restroom' and noticed a handwritten note on the wall close to the lavatory door; it read 'Customers who find our waitresses rude ought to see the manager'. I laughed out loud. I wasn't sure if it was a clever play on words or just poorly written, either way it brightened my day. Actually the waitress had been charming and very understanding of our need to shelter from the rain.

During a break in the rain we made a bit of a dash for it and found a perfect place to pitch the tent for the night, out of sight of everything but equally close enough to everything we wanted. Feeling a little lazy and clean out of Dinty Moore we visited a Pizza Hut to refuel our calorific craving. This might have been 'foreign' food, but from tomorrow onwards it was going to be a serious challenge for my weak constitution as we were going to Mexico. I had horrible visions of what I might come across there in terms of inedible food. I dreaded the thought of ghastly over-spiced, undercooked rancid meat, in a greasy foul-stanching sauce. The very thought of it filled me with horror.

We ran back to the tent as the rain fell again and

got a sound night's sleep while it belted down outside.

Still raining the following morning, we packed up best we could and headed downtown. I made a point of eating a very hearty lunch and then caught a bus over the border into Juarez. We found a local bank and exchanged our dollars for pesos at 22.6. We had no idea if that was good or not. We headed for the train station and bought a ticket to Chihuahua. The super-fast speedy express left three hours late and eventually rolled into Chihuahua after 9p.m. A bloke on the train had suggested a 'good value' hotel, so we went with a licensed bandit in a taxi to find the hotel. Having been ripped off by the bandito, the hotel receptionist asked us for 200 pesos or nearly nine bucks for the night. We stood our ground and said no way, especially for this shithole. After a bit of a heated argument we agreed 300 for two nights.

Tuesday morning we bought our first meal in Mexico, a very poor quality chicken and chips. It didn't cost much but wasn't much good either. The town of Chihuahua was nice, with a few flashy shops with a classic Roman Catholic church at the heart of the town, but it was very apparent the infrastructure suffered from lack of investment and there were beggars on every street corner. We watched some kids kicking, what looked like from afar, a deflated football. It didn't bounce at all and was an odd shape. As we got closer we realised with some revulsion it was actually a severed cow's head skidding and sliding across the potholed tarmac. Its bloodied chewed eye-sockets were covered in flies: I felt like throwing up. The local butcher had thrown it in a bin only for it to have been scavenged by a wild dog that had done his best to gnaw on the pathetic emancipated skull and then abandoned it in the street for the kids to find and play with. This pathetic disparity between third-world Mexico and the wealthiest country in the world just a few hours away was stark for all to see; but only if you are looking. Feeling more than a bit humbled and repulsed by the cow's head episode we had decided to go on to Los Mochis, but enquiring back at the train station found out there wasn't a train for two days.

We stocked up on some grub from a modernish looking supermarket and headed back to the hotel for the evening. Whatever we were eating was very spicy and neither Steve nor I could stop farting, it was like a scene from *Blazing Saddles*! God, the room stank that night.

Wednesday we kicked about town, not really knowing what to do with ourselves. We looked into a grotty-looking bar where there was one lone European propping up the bar. He introduced himself as Heinz from Dusseldorf. He told us for the past two years he had been travelling the world and showed us the stamps in his passport to prove it. He really had been everywhere, apart from all the normal European countries including Scandinavia, he had been to the Middle East and south-east Asia, Australia and New Zealand and a fair chunk of Africa and across to South America. This was one impressive guy and made us feel like rank amateurs, which we were. Heinz was well educated and could speak four or five languages including Spanish, which was very useful in Mexico. We had a couple of beers with him and agreed to meet up later at a café/bar he recommended. We arrived at six and Heinz introduced us to a French girl he had met a couple of days earlier. Over the next few hours we were joined by a Flemish guy from Belgium, a French-Canadian bloke, a Brit called Rod Slater and finally another German girl, Renate. It was one of those spontaneous nights where everybody just clicked and we had great fun swapping stories of our travels with each other – even the food was good and pitchers of beer just kept on arriving.

At 7a.m. next morning we took a taxi back to Chihuahua station and settled down for a very long day on the train. At one point we went along the top of a breathtaking canyon which a local Mexican senorita told us it was called Copper Canyon and was in fact longer and deeper than the Grand Canyon. It was certainly as equally beautiful. It was such a shame we rattled on along its southern rim without stopping. The lady said it was Mexico's best kept secret; here was an outstanding natural feature which the authorities chose to ignore, while in the USA the Grand Canyon was a marketing man's dream to punt to the tourists.

It took forever to arrive at Los Mochis, although we had travelled through eighty-six tunnels and over thirty bridges and we only had a short time to take a quick look about before transferring trains to head south to Tepic. The train left at midnight and it was standing room only so Stevie and I dossed in the bottom compartment of a luggage rack and had people treading on our legs all night. We got up at seven and managed to find some empty seats for the remainder of the excruciatingly slow journey to San Blas. There had been a French trio babbling away all night (obviously in French) who were really getting on our nerves. Everyone was trying to sleep – it had been a long night – so Stevie went straight up to them and, finding an inner courage I didn't know he possessed, looked them straight in the eye and said, 'Will you shut up for fuck sake and go to sleep or just piss off to another carriage.' Neither he nor I had any idea if they understood him, but we never heard another word from them for the rest of the journey.

We had to take a bus from Tepic for the last leg of the journey down to San Blas, but had an hour or so to kill and migrated towards the main town plaza. There before us stood a magnificent cathedral built in a neo-gothic architectural form with two enormous matching bell towers. The Catedral de Purisima Concepcion (Immaculate Conception Cathedral) was without question the most amazing architecture I had seen in the last five months. It was such a shame we didn't make time to have a really good look round, but we didn't want to miss the bus onto San Blas.

I had stupidly bought a carton of prawns from a vendor walking down the train earlier and now was seriously starting to regret it. On arrival at San Blas I was violently sick behind the bus station. I drank down a litre of bottled water and gradually felt better. We found a cheapish hotel just off the main plaza and booked in for the night. We stumbled across a Mexican bar, the 'La Hacienda', complete with cockroaches and smoking Chimenea. I suspected we were on a well-worn travel route when we linked up in no time with an American couple from California, Jaxon and Sarah, and two Dutch girls from Zwolle. The bar was timeless and I suspected it wouldn't have looked too much different had we passed through a hundred years before. I managed to eat some burritos, but after the prawn incident didn't feel much like anything.

After a very basic breakfast of bread and strong coffee the next morning, Stevie and I met up with the Dutch lasses, Mila and Millie by arrangement and caught a bus out of town where we took a boat ride through a dense jungle and mangroves. We finished up at a clear water lagoon and swam for an hour. We met an Anglo-American Mexican guy there who went by the name of Jay Sentosa. Although a Mexican by birth he had lived in New York and had been to university in the UK. A real man of the world and it showed. He was a fountain of knowledge and very helpful to us all. He wore a fantastic T-shirt which read:

Heaven: Is where the police are British: the cooks are Italian:
The mechanics are German: the lovers are French and
Everything is organised by the Swiss

Hell: Is where the police are German: the cooks are American:
The mechanics are French: the lovers are Swiss and
Everything is organised by the Italians

The Mila and Millie girls were most offended the Dutch didn't feature in either category, which as he blandly pointed out may say something about the Dutch! I would have given Jay every peso I had for his T-shirt (not that I had many), but it was not for sale. Jay pointed us to the beach, which was like something out of a Lunn Poly holiday brochure; a serious picture postcard beach. San Blas Beach was about three miles long with pure light-yellow sand backed by dense foliage and palm trees. This was possibly as close to paradise as I would ever get. There were barely ten people on the entire beach, I put my arm round Millie's shoulders but felt her rejection immediately. I ran into the rolling waves to escape my disappointment and embarrassment. Stevie joined me in the water and said, 'Haven't you worked it out yet? They're a butch couple, together, lezzyies, lesbians.'

'Oh Christ, I hadn't realised, never gave it a thought.' I decided to go back on the beach to tackle this head on and said sorry to Millie, who dismissed it and said, 'I should apologise to you, I am flattered you should think of me that way.'

'Well no hard feelings and no offence meant,' I reiterated. She looked bashful and to my surprise kissed me.

'No offence taken!' I wasn't going to hold their sexuality against them they were nice girls and good company. Bloody shame though, she could really kiss! Lucky bloody Mila was all I could think.

Early evening back in San Blas we bumped into our Californian drinking buddies from last night and they let us know of a campsite they had discovered no more than a mile from the central plaza. It was half the price of the hotel so we made an immediate switch of accommodation. We all met back at the 'La Hacienda' including Millie and Mila, and sat mesmerised as a Mexican wedding parade crossed the plaza with over a hundred people dressed up in their best wedding suits and frocks, despite the searing heat. The cockroaches seemed to have doubled in number since yesterday, but despite that this tavern did have a magic charm, the beer was cold and drinkable and the food passable.

Woke up Sunday morning not feeling too great and passing through the passable food. I had a burning throat and was feeling weak. I guess the cockroaches had given fair warning last night. I only had twenty-five pesos to last me all day until the banks opened tomorrow, so despite feeling grotty I wandered back to the plaza and bought some coffee for breakfast and oranges and bananas for lunch. Around midday with Jaxon and Sarah, Mila and Millie we caught an absolute bone-rattler of a bus, minus suspension, a beat-up old engine, belching toxic black smoke and went back to the same beach as yesterday. The ride hadn't helped my stomach settle down and I had to run to the nearest tree much to Stevie's amusement. Virtually the first, indeed only person we met was Jay Sentosa. He was wearing yet another sensational T-shirt. This one had a faded Union Jack with the words:

1943: UK Utility Knickers

'One Yank and they're off'
I don't know where this guy bought his T-shirts, but I thought they were absolutely brilliant. The Dutch girls didn't get it and I wasn't completely sure Jaxon did either.

Jay had a large surfboard with him. I asked what he did and he told us he was a sort of self-appointed independent San Blas tour guide/surfboard instructor as and when he wanted to be. He just shrugged and said, 'Living my dream, man; much like you guys. I came by here a few years back and fell in love with the place and never left.'

We sunbathed for four hours despite still feeling rough and got back to the campsite and effectively went to bed at 5.30 as I was feeling rotten and just sweated it out. As Groucho would say, 'I had a wonderful day – but this wasn't it!'

Fortunately I was feeling a lot better come Monday morning and headed to the bank to exchange some traveller's cheques. They said they couldn't do that due to pending fluctuations in the exchange rate. Very helpful. I had to wait it out for three hours before they were willing to do the exchange. By that time Stevie said he wasn't feeling too well and returned to the tent to rest up. I was feeling better and better so, with nothing else planned, I went back to the beach. It really was paradise, the sun blazed down and the waves rolled in and I had utopia exclusively all to myself all day. The next day, with Stevie and I returned to full health, we decided to hitchhike to Guadalajara (the only time we hitched in Mexico). It took a few hours to nail down a lift, but a couple of very well-to-do locals gave us a lift most of the way in a brand-new sedan car. Upon arrival we booked into a crappy hotel and went out for a quite awful and indescribable dinner, which we felt was a rip-off. Priced menus weren't too common and we got the firm impression the waiters pitched for as much they could get. Gringos were seen as fair game, so the prices started high. Unfortunately we made the classic mistake of not asking about the price until it was too late. We would remember that in future and try and find somewhere a little more upmarket.

Guadalajara is Mexico's second largest city, so changing hotels that morning was not a problem. Stuffed full of neo-Gothic churches and cathedrals, some upmarket shopping and plenty of flea markets; Guadalajara was a very easy place to spend your money as generally everything was such good value. We found a shop that looked like Harrods at Woolworths prices and bought a few small gifts for family to take home. Late afternoon we walked into the Sheraton Hotel and bought a half-decent supper for a lot less than last night's garbage.

I had seen a billboard for a football match tonight between Guadalajara Tecos and Veracruz. It was played at the stadium where Gordon Banks made his finest ever save from Pele in the 1970 World Cup. There wasn't a large crowd but it was simply one of the finest football matches I had ever seen live. The skill level and speed of these Mexican players was like nothing I had ever seen before. I thought it was a terrific spectacle and entertainment.

Stevie complained of feeling unwell and left the

ground very early.

I returned to the hotel only to discover Steve was not there; I was concerned as to where the hell he was or if anything had happened to him. At 3a.m. he came back and said he had been to hospital and he was shit scared he might have caught some awful tropical disease such as dengue or yellow fever. He probably had flu or a bit of food poisoning; but to be on the safe side a doctor had given him an injection on the bum. Showing a complete lack of empathy, compassion and solidarity, I couldn't stop laughing at Steve's misfortune and paranoia.

The doctor had suggested to Steve that I should also administer a series of injections up his bum and sent him back to the hotel with a bag full of disposable hypodermic syringes, complete with a hand-drawn map of a posterior with an 'X' marking the target area. Neither of us could really believe it; suffice to say we didn't want anything to do with it.

'I'm not letting you anywhere near my backside with that thing,' Steve said firmly.

'Fine by me, mate, I have no desire to be anywhere near your arse,' I retorted. It could have been a course of anti-biotics; we would never know. What I do know is he made a remarkably swift recovery from whatever it was (probably in his head).

I love old architecture and Guadalajara did not disappoint as it was crammed full of old Spanish colonial buildings. Old buildings and classical architecture were the one thing the USA could not produce for obvious reasons, which explains why the small percentage of Americans that do travel abroad are so besotted with Europe. It was built in the past;

a past that America has never enjoyed.

Having given the Sheraton a five-star approval yesterday we thought it a fairly safe bet to return to for a late lunch and then went off to visit the city's oldest flea market, the El Baratillo Mercado. It was a gigantic market selling everything under the sun from old electrical junk, to bed linens to jewellery, to rip-off fake branded clothing such as Levi's which clearly weren't, to Aztec handicrafts to street food to books and luggage bags. Haggling was the name of the game. I was particularly amused when browsing at a stall, another stallholder opposite shouted out to us 'Hey amigo, come over to my stall and let me rip you off instead.' With a sales patter like that he was bound to go far! A sixteen-year-old girl, who could have passed for twenty made a beeline for us and flirted for some time. I was uncomfortable with her, as pretty and polite as she was. She may have been genuinely interested in us as foreign visitors, but I just had a feeling it would be in our best interests to walk away. She looked disappointed when we said goodbye and sure enough a shady character appeared from nowhere and admonished her. I don't know if he was a pimp or a parent or maybe both, but I felt we were being set up and she was undoubtedly being exploited. I was pleased when Steve said he thought exactly the same, which kind of vindicated my thinking.

We'd bought a few great value items to take home, from keepsakes to new shirts and shoes. The issue we both had was space and weight in our backpacks. So we made a big decision to dump our gas cooker, saucepan, plates and mugs. We hadn't used them for a while and predicted we wouldn't miss them too much. Clearly this also committed us to eating out every day with the associated cost implication, but the added benefit of never having to eat Dinty Moore Stew ever again, which really was the winning vote! So with some ceremony we put everything we no longer wanted in a plastic bag and dumped it in a public litter bin in downtown Guadalajara.

The next few days followed a similar pattern with the Sheraton becoming a main feeding den and the city markets and streets keeping us occupied during the day.

On Sunday 5th November we caught a bus to Mexico City which took eleven hours to complete. Neither of us were fans of coach travel but short of hitchhiking, which we had been strongly advised not to do by just about everyone we spoke to, coach travel was the best value mode of transport. We could travel two thirds the length of the country for $5, so we decided to get down to Acapulco the following morning – a further six-and-a-half hours – to put the lion's share of the coach travel behind us. Maybe it wasn't such a good idea, as for six-and-a-half hours we endured screaming kids and crying babies while their moronic mothers seemed oblivious to the noise and tantrums. As we didn't arrive until 8.30p.m. we let a local 'guide' drive us to a so-called hotel. This prison cell had to be seen to be believed. The room had no window, no towels, no shaving mirror, no loo roll, no anything. The proprietor who looked like a bandito, indeed I think he was a bandito, suggested fifty pesos. Steve spotted a dirty great cockroach scuttle under one of the beds. I pointed to a beetle on the wall. We offered twenty pesos for one night, including the free cockroach and beetle. We agreed twenty-five!

We left the prison cell first thing in the morning and headed down to Caleta Beach. We found a good enough hotel, at least it was a proper hotel; if not top end it was the best in which we had stayed in Mexico to date. We were told despite the ideal outdoor temperature of about 85 degrees it was 'out of season' and the prices reflected this to seduce the non-existent tourists. After a long afternoon on the beach we went into downtown Acapulco and discovered the best restaurant in town for American food was F W Woolworths. Back home Woolworths was a multi-purpose department store selling low-priced housewares, electricals and records. Here in Mexico it stocked fashion clothes, a restaurant and a coffee shop. Back at Caleta we had a couple of beers at a beach-front bar and hit the sack. We needed a good night's sleep after last night's stay in prison. On Wednesday morning we made a point of having a good look around Acapulco and spent the afternoon on the beach. In fact we spent more time in the water than on the beach; it was so warm and good. We ate at a shack off the beach then decided to invest a hundred pesos to go on an all-inclusive night-time cruise on a large yacht with an abundance of sails, called the *Hawauana*. While sailing right around Acapulco Bay and out to Roqueta Island we fell into a very interesting conversation with a Guatemalan guy and two beauties from Hawaii. After copious amounts of beer, rum and cokes/gin and orange, we arrived back at 2.00 the following morning. I vaguely recall we all had a nightcap in the hotel bar. Proudly displayed on the bar was a framed notice in Mexican English: 'Ladies are requested not to have children in the bar'. And say so all of us. I was hoping to wake up in the arms of one of the Hawaiian Goddesses, but was disappointed to find myself back at our room alone with Stevie snoring his head off lying stark bollock naked the wrong way across his bed. Talk about disappointment!

The one thing hotels here never seem to offer is breakfast as part of the package. They see it as an extra opportunity to take advantage of your custom and loyalty and then rip you off.

Wandering around the back streets we came across a small square with an empty café. We sat down and ordered coffee. A greasy looking chap wearing a filthy white apron asked us if we would like to order breakfast and handed us a sticky plastic handwritten menu card with no prices on.

I said, 'OK, how much for three rashers of bacon, sausage, two fried eggs, mushrooms and tomatoes and toast.' He said, 'Thirty pesos, señor.'

Steve said 'Demasiado (*too much*). How about no sausage and no tomatoes. How much would that be?'

Señor Greasy said, 'Thirty pesos, señor.'

'It can't be,' exclaimed Stevie, 'it has gotta be less as there's gonna be less on the plate, so the price has to go down. How about twenty-five pesos?'

'Na, thirty pesos señor.'

I thought I would have a go at reasoning with the

stubborn waiter, 'Tell you what, we need you to reduce the price; so we'll just have eggs, bacon and toast, forget the rest. How much?'

'Thirty pesos señor. Breakfast is set price whatever you have.'

'Not where we come from. At the Wimpey if you don't order it, you don't pay for it,' said Stevie. With that we stood up to go.

Señor Greasy, seeing his only customers of the day about to desert him suddenly decided to negotiate. 'I have the Breakfast of the Day Special,' he grandly announced. There was no written sign of this 'Special' anywhere in the square, the café or the table. I just looked at him somewhat exasperated.

'Scrambled egg and bacon, just twenty pesos, señor.'

'Oh really,' said Steve incredulously, 'does that include unlimited coffee and toast?' Señor Greasy was on the back foot now. He mumbled and spluttered a bit in colourful Mexican before nodding in agreement and disappeared indoors to his kitchen.

'For Christsakes,' said Stevie, 'you wouldn't believe it could be so hard to buy a friggin breakfast,' then burst in to uncontrollable laughter.

I loved haggling, but Señor Greasy had really wound me up as it was obvious he charged whatever he thought he could get away with. I struggled to find the humour in it.

Later we took a ferry out to Roqueta Island and spent a long afternoon on the beach there. After dinner at Woolworths we went to see the high rock diving, which Acapulco is famed for. A kid of not more than fifteen dived 132 feet with a flaming torch in each hand. It was all pretty spectacular. The next couple of days followed a similar pattern of beaches, sunshine, swimming and Woolworths dinners.

We returned to Mexico City by coach and fortunately the backward journey was a lot quieter than the trip down here. We stumbled across the Hotel Polly and booked in for three nights at 400 pesos. It was a bland, bulk standard two-star central hotel with no stand out features. Having checked in, I looked at the notice board for any restaurant recommendations. There weren't any. However there was another great example of Mexican English. A typed-up laminated notice which stated: 'Because of the impropriety of entertaining guests of the opposite sex in the bedrooms, it is suggested that the lobby be used for this purpose'!

We took the new Mexico metro train right into the heart of the city and stepped out to see one of the largest posters I'd ever seen. Measuring at least 100 feet by 60 feet, it was advertising this year's blockbuster movie *Grease* starring John Travolta and Olivia Newton John, except in Mexico it was billed as *La Vaselina*, which we found quite funny. We had seen the movie in fact in San Diego with Becky and Rachael. It was good wholesome family entertainment and a great sing-a-long movie. We bought an American-style hamburger and found the best pastry shop in Latin America.

Bullfighting in Mexico is the National sport, and billboard posters advertising the bullfights were on every street corner. The matadors have God-like status and are treated just as rock stars or American football players are in the States. We decided we would go along to see this extraordinary primitive cultural tradition and headed along to the bullring. There were four 'fights' on the bill. They were all bloody, inhumane and repulsive and yet the crowd went into a frenzy with each stab of a spear, dart or sword. Just to goad the dumb creatures the matador attached four or five darts to the bull's torso, then for good measure stuck a spear in the rump. Finally the sword is used for the final act of indignation and dissolution. I guess bullfighting would be alright if the bull could use a sword too. The second fight was graded as 'good' and the matador being awarded the bull's ear – charming! It really turned my stomach to watch this cruel and barbaric spectacle. However, the last fight the matador had his comeuppance when the bull tossed him into the air and he landed on his back; the bull sped forward to gnaw the prostrate matador. Stevie and I, now on our feet, cheered on the bull much to the disgust of the crowd around us, as up to six other matadors ran at the bull with their spears to keep him at bay. Now with a seven-one advantage the senior matador went for the kill and raised his sword for the final deathly thrust. We booed loudly as the crowd around us hissed and glared their contempt for the two uninitiated gringos. OK, if this is how Mexicans get their kicks, and then in my view they are very sick. The problem with the average man is he thinks he isn't and this lot was well below average! They were just a blood-thirsty bunch of sadistic and malevolent morons. Change the names from Mexicans to Romans, bulls to Christians, matadors to lions and bullring to colosseum and nothing has changed much in two thousand years. I couldn't wait to leave and vowed never ever again to support such a pitiful and uncivilised blood sport.

I had lost my appetite last night so awoke this morning a little hungry and went to the 'Big Burger' for breakfast. This certainly wasn't ideal, but at least I could eat it and it filled a void. We then took the metro out to Chapultepec Park on the west side of Mexico City to see the many attractions, waterfalls, lakes and general beauty of the park. To our surprise we walked into Rod Slater who we had briefly met in Chihuahua a couple of weeks back. He said he had travelled right down to the Caribbean coast of Belize. We all wandered around together and decided to go the cinema early evening to see *MacArthur* with Gregory Peck. At ten pesos it was excellent value and a damn good film too. Later we found a downtown bar and talked ate and drank for three hours.

Rod was an interesting bloke of about twenty-six and a qualified surveyor, he lived somewhere in Cheshire and worked for the district valuer's office in Central Manchester. Lack of money wasn't a problem for him.

I asked Rod, 'Why did you specifically go to Belize?' Rod said he wanted to see the 'Great Blue Hole'. I asked him what that was exactly.

'Have you not heard of it?'

'No.'

'I shouldn't be surprised; I haven't met anyone outside of Belize who has. Well it's a large round blue well about fifty miles off the Caribbean coast; it is one of nature's remarkable wonders of the world. It is actually a marine sink hole, which plunges 400 feet down into the ocean bed in the middle of the barrier reef. It's a perfect circular shape measuring about a thousand feet across.'

As it seems no one knew anything about it, I asked, 'How did you find out about it?'

'Ah well my main passion is diving, you know scuba diving. I read about it in diving magazine a year or two back. I'd always wanted to come to this part of the world, so decided to spend some time in Mexico and Central America and the Great Blue Hole was top of my diving list. If you look at aerial pictures of it, it looks like a deep blue pond surface in the middle of the sea. It really drew me in.'

Rod showed us a couple of postcards he'd bought of it. We could see the appeal.

'How did you get out there? Is it dangerous down there?' chipped in Steve.

'Belize is not as chaotic as you might imagine. Firstly they still come under British jurisdiction, even though British Honduras no longer exists. Technically the Queen is still head of state. English is officially the first language although Belize Créole is commonly spoken. The Blue Hole is actually their biggest tourist attraction, and I knew I would be able to hire all the diving gear I needed. Boats take tourists and divers out from Belize City all the time – you should go, it was really worth the effort and cost.'

'Is it expensive?' I asked.

'Cheap as chips. The most expensive part by far was the British Airways return flight to Mexico City.'

'Where else have you been since Chihuahua?'

'I went to Guadalajara and then directly down to Guatemala for a few days and on to Belize for a week. Spent a couple of nights in Yucatan as I wanted to visit the Mayan pyramid of Chichen Itza, it was pretty awesome. I arrived back here two days ago and fly home tomorrow.'

'Wow sounds bloody fantastic,' I said with a pang of envy.

We told him we had also been to Guadalajara, and may have overlapped by a day and told him about the Acapulco beach and rock diving and the bloody barbaric bullfight.

Rod had been intriguing to talk to and very thought provoking. However, we had plans to go back up to the States and agreed not to be deflected. The Great Blue Hole would have to wait.

Wednesday 15th November we took the 8a.m. train from Mexico City up to Nuevo Laredo on the banks of the Rio Grande and US border. It was a boring and unpleasant journey for the most part, as a succession of old women and kids constantly walked up and down the carriages selling smelly stale tacos, refried beans and other crappy foods. I had no idea what was actually in these tacos but it was nothing I recognised! I decided I would rather starve than eat this dross. Fortunately we had brought with us a couple of bottles of water and vacuum-sealed sandwiches. We were midway up the carriage and as far from the toilet as possible and yet all I could smell was the acrid pong from the urinal in addition to the awful tacos. Fortunately both Steve and I managed to keep a spare seat beside us for the entire journey and slept on and off through the night. We arrived at Nuevo Laredo at 09.30 the next morning and went straight across the border to Laredo, Texas as fast as we could.

13. Dixieland, Hannah The Hooker and The DC Dilemma!

We knew we were running down the clock on our marathon journey and our cash was leaking away despite Mexico being incredibly cheap for us. We were also aware that as we travelled north up the east coast the weather would deteriorate as we headed towards December. We made a decision on the train to see if we could track down a deal with the Greyhound buses and travel with a bit more certainty and comfort. We got lucky; we 'done a deal' and agreed a fifteen-day Greyhound pass for $65 each. It came with time restrictions, but we figured if we travelled at night we would save on hotels expenses and not waste the days. However, within twenty minutes we took a coach to San Antonio, arriving late afternoon. We checked-in our backpacks at the left luggage counter and headed straight out to see the Alamo Mission.

Being of historical and architectural interest, I found it fascinating and was delighted to look about and take it all in. I sometimes felt Stevie in these situations just came along out of curiosity, but didn't share my sense of awe either for the history or architecture. In this case I gave him absolutely no choice as the Battle of the Alamo, 1836 was something I had studied at Hasting College FE and was on my must-see list. We grabbed a pizza and made our way back to the Greyhound station and boarded a coach to Houston, which departed at 11.30p.m. We arrived at Houston Bus station at 03.45

and with nowhere to go sat it out in the terminal until 08.00, but just couldn't sleep. By 8.30 we found ourselves a dirt-cheap hotel, possibly even worse than the Windsor in San Francisco and went straight to bed and slept through to 4p.m. Venturing out we took a look around the downtown area. The city was absolutely crammed full of skyscrapers and tower blocks constructed of steel and glass, which dazzled in the sun. It was all too late to do anything really so we bought a takeaway burger and went back to our dive.

We wanted to have a day in Houston, but try as we might to find something interesting to see or do we struggled to occupy the day. Early afternoon we went to the Galleria shopping mall; generally these places leave me cold, but I had to admit this one was as good as any I had been to in six months. We spent a good few hours browsing record shops and book stores. There was a cinema at the Galleria showing *Wild Geese* with Roger Moore – I sound like him apparently – plus Richard Burton and Richard Harris. With all those Richards and Rogers we decided to go and see it. The box office was shuttered up but the film was screening so we just walked in for free. I wasn't sure if that was the idea; there was no one to ask anyhow. After a couple of beers and a 'submarine' we returned to the drab Greyhound terminal and booked an overnight coach to New Orleans. I felt we hadn't done justice to Houston, but apart from the skyline and *Wild Geese* I really wasn't sure what else to see.

New Orleans was another ball game altogether. We

had heard good things about 'the Big Easy' and in my view most of what I had heard had been understated. The city had a real vibe and character, lacking in so many of America's larger cities. We rolled into town as the sun came up and were immediately struck as to how different it was. Its long-lost French heritage still influenced the place names, the architecture and ambience. I asked at the Greyhound info centre if they could recommend a place to stay and they pointed us to a hotel several blocks down the road. The Dixieland Hotel looked pretty good and charged accordingly; begrudgingly we paid for a couple of nights. By mid-morning we were in the French Quarter and the famous Bourbon Street where it is said jazz originated. Over in Canal Street it had a real French-style café culture about it, I suspect not seen anywhere else in the USA. We sat down outside a French style Patisserie with a cup of coffee and doughnuts, as a long loud carnival procession streamed past. We were told by a guy from upstate Louisiana these were virtually daily parades. Frankly both Stevie and I were blown away, it was just wonderful to be here and feel a part of something we could really identify with – and the day was only just beginning. After a fairly lengthy siesta during the afternoon back at the hotel, we got ready for a proper Saturday evening out and hit the jazz clubs. We were becoming a bit reckless with our money, but having stinted for the best part of six months we were ready to splash out a bit. We had a classic southern dinner at Papa Joe's Steak House, where we had the full sirloin with gumbo and sweet potato fries. I had no idea what was in the sauce, but

I really enjoyed it. Stevie commented that I was questioning foreign food less by the day. That was maybe true, but unlike Mexico this stuff was very edible! Afterwards we went to a series of different jazz clubs, all of which were free if you were buying beer. Every one of them was just fantastic; I don't think I had ever quite experienced an atmosphere like it. The jazz and blues filled the room as the beers went down. People were so friendly and interesting to talk to, not just about music but anything at all. This was true Dixieland and frankly was probably the best night I had out in six months and that was despite some pretty strong competition along the way. I know one thing, 03.50 was the latest time I had ever gone to bed!

A note was waiting for me under the door when I returned to the Dixieland Hotel from a lady of the night suggesting I gave her a call. Well, no way and I was far too knackered for that anyhow. I crashed out instantaneously. Four hours later there was a loud knocking on the door, I staggered in my underwear to see who it was to find a woman not wearing too much, looking sultry and sexy standing there. 'Hi there, good looking, I'm Naughty Nicola,' she said. I looked behind me: there was no one there. 'Yeah?' I blurted, rubbing my eyes. She handed me a card with her rates on. I handed it back and slammed the door in her face. I thought this was a classy joint at $25 a night. I think if she been included in the price I would have still slammed the door in her face. She shouted a stream of abuse at me from outside the door and knocked on the door to the room next to me. It just wasn't gonna be her night, as Stevie was so zonked out he didn't even hear her knock!

Despite the uninvited interruption, I did actually have a good night's sleep and at twelve found myself back in the Canal Street for more coffee and doughnuts. Unlike Houston, information centres were plentiful in the Mardi Gras City. Stevie made the point that New Orleans had plenty to shout about which was reflected in the tourist trade which evidently Houston did not. We picked up a leaflet about an authentic Mississippi paddle steamer and caught a bus out to see it. For a few bucks we could take a ride and look around the boat. They were unique to the river and designed specifically for the shallow parts of the Mississippi river. Developed in the early part of the nineteenth century they were originally of wood construction, with either a large rear rotating paddle or two side paddles, driven by enormous steam engines and boilers, fuelled predominately by coal. Originally they transported goods such as timber, tobacco and cotton from the Gulf up as far as was navigable. After the 1830s when the South had joined the Union and navigation had improved, they could reach as far north as Pittsburgh and Ohio in seven days with commerce trading in both directions. By the 1840s it was estimated there were as many as a thousand-plus paddle steamers competing for commercial contracts and river domination. The biggest issue the steamers had was a combination of excessive use, combined with poor workmanship causing boiler explosions, which led to mass fatalities.

Rigorous legislation in the mid-nineteenth century tightened things up alongside the conversion to steel hulls.

After the American Civil War, showboats had been introduced which were nothing more than floating theatres. These actually weren't paddle steamers, but were pulled by tugs. They couldn't have operated with a huge steam engine, as it would have had to have been placed in the middle of the auditorium! Gambling was rife on these boats as they floated between states without accountability. Arguably the river showboats were the first form of modern-day cruise entertainment in the world.

Back on terra firma we knew we wouldn't better last night, but we were keen to give it another go and returned to the French Quarter. We found ourselves at Preservation Hall and watched and listened to the 'Sweet Emma Barrett Jazz Band'. They were a seven-piece band of old timers playing trad jazz and blues and possibly the best value for a dollar I would ever have. These guys were real polished pros, who just lived for their craft and were incredible. There was a shortish squat fella with an enormous pot belly which made him look like a buddha; he was propped up against his double base. The grizzled old fella on guitar looked a hundred. He had a sublime touch; if I closed my eyes I could have sworn it was B.B. King. He was so craggy his face looked like a map of the Mississippi Delta, but what the hell did it matter what he looked like when you could play like that? We listened to a two-hour set and knew we had been privileged to witness something special.

We went on to another club where a modern jazz saxophonist was playing, called Gary Brown. He was out of this world, the best of the lot. I had always been a huge fan of the sax; I just loved the sound and tone of them. Mayall always featured horn players on his Blues Breakers albums. Sax legends such as Dick Heckstall-Smith, Chris Mercer, Johnny Almond, Clifford Solomon and Ernie Watts had me hooked on this remarkable reed instrument. Some may think it sad, but these guys were my heroes along with the Grateful Dead, Tony Greig and Julie Andrews!

We stayed and listened to Gary for a couple of hours. During a break I introduced myself to him and asked if he had cut any recordings we could buy. His reply astounded me:

'As a matter of fact I do I have a single out right now; it's number one in the charts over in England. It is the theme to *Grease* the movie; I'm the sax player on it.' We couldn't believe it, the sax player from *La Vaselina*! I was speechless. Gary was so modest and unassuming, shrugged his shoulders as though it was no big deal; I just hoped he was getting good royalties. Stevie said he thought the theme to *Grease* was one with Frankie Valli singing vocals. I wasn't sure.

Gary went back on stage to start the next set and said, 'Ladies and gentleman we have two special guests in the club tonight, two big jazz fans – Steve and Richard from London, England. You are very welcome in New Orleans.' We were actually applauded! I was glad it was dark as I could feel myself going bright red out of complete embarrassment.

On our last day in New Orleans we went back into

tourist mode and went to parks and the New Orleans Super Dome and the State Library, where I was pleased to find a copy of yesterday's *Sunday Times* from London. It seemed that Brighton had lost again! Before returning to the Greyhound bus station we had one last look at a jazz club on Bourbon Street had a light meal and beer, and drank in the aura and emotion of the jazz. It was hard to tear ourselves away, but go we must.

Ever since we started out back in May, Florida was always on the list of US States to visit; Miami, the Everglades and the Keys were a must-visit. I knew people from home who said it was a fantastic holiday destination. However, reality was setting in. We didn't have the money and time was running out. Deep down I knew as soon as we decided to detour into Mexico, something would have to give, so with deep misgivings we decided to give up Florida and make for Richmond, via Atlanta and Charlotte, a not inconsiderable distance of about a thousand miles. We had to change buses a couple of times. At the Atlanta Greyhound depot, Steve left his red windcheater jacket on the back of a seat in the coffee bar. We had only moved barely forty feet, but when Stevie returned for it, it had been pinched. It was a long and uncomfortable twenty-four-hour ride which, as it turned out, was a bit pointless. We phoned Tom and Pat who we had met way back on the other side of the continent on Vancouver Island; they had been insistent we look them up and stay, only to find they were out of town for a few days. The weather was foul, torrential rain and freezing cold and in Steve's case, no jacket any longer. Feeling more than a little pissed off and wishing we had just been bolder and gone to Fort Lauderdale, we discussed options before agreeing to go on to Washington DC, a further hundred miles up the highway. We knew we would have to cut out more than we wanted to here in the east, but DC was not negotiable; we had to go there.

The bus was busy with only a few spare seats available so I sat next to a very attractive blonde and made the usual small talk. Instantly she wanted to know if I was Australian. I told her it was a lot better than that and I was in fact British. She gave me a vacant smile; I suspected she didn't know the difference between the two countries or indeed where either was in the world. I wasn't about to tell her. We exchanged names; she was Hannah and I asked her what she did.

'I hang around bars mainly,' she said matter-of-factually. I was a bit slow and wondered if she meant she poured drinks behind the bar.

'I like men and women,' she added. Slowly it dawned on me.

'Oh,' I said, not quite knowing if I should say any more. Really what could I say? She was a rampant bi-sexual prostitute and I was a green behind the ears, naïve foolishly credulous embarrassed Brit, who was unusually stuck for words. She could see right through me.

'Don't be embarrassed,' she said, 'I am what I am. I love sex. I love men. I love women and I love money. It all goes together very well for me.' The girl had no shame, I suspected she wasn't really a lesbian either; she just ran out of men occasionally!

'So why are you going to DC?' I asked her.

'Returning home. Just been to see my mam in Richmond for a few days.' I didn't want to ask what her mother thought of her occupation, so didn't reply. 'Why you going to DC?' she asked.

'Well me and Stevie back there, are on our way back to New York and thought we'd spend a few days in Washington and do the tourist thing.' I was going to add we had also hitchhiked six or seven thousand miles but assumed I was boring her now as she slowly nodded and kept quiet. She quietly closed her eyes. After about five minutes she perked up and said, 'If you visit the Presidents Bar on 8th & 14th on Thursday, Thanksgiving Day, I'll seeya there. Maybe we could have a good time, Richard. It could be fun.'

It could be a big mistake too, I thought. I made a mental note to steer clear of 8th & 14th and the Presidents Bar.

'Probably not, Hannah,' I stupidly blurted out.

'Huh? You don't like me?' she said moodily. I decided not to dig a hole any deeper and kept quiet myself for a while.

'Tell me about Thanksgiving, Hannah. It's not something we have in the UK.'

'Oh it's just an excuse for a party. Everyone takes the day off and gets drunk. The big cities normally have street processions and carnivals. Family dinners of roast turkey and parties are fairly traditional. Personally I find it a good pay day!' Christ this girl really was insatiable and so forthright, she made me laugh.

243

'I bet,' I said. 'You have come alive again, Hannah.'

'Next mood swing; five minutes,' she replied with a deadpan face.

We arrived in Washington and Stevie said he had shared his seat with 'two-ton Ted from Lexington'. This bloody bloke snored the whole journey long and nearly pushed me off the seat a couple of times.' I told him about Hannah and Thanksgiving.

'Well, I would be tempted,' said Steve. 'She is absolutely gorgeous.'

'That she is, mate, but she will bonk you, charge you and probably infect you!'

Hannah was out of sight and soon a distant and somewhat amusing encounter, now gone forever. A guy at the bus station pointed us to the youth hostel in the Foggy Bottom area of town, which was about all we could afford. It was surprisingly good, clean and excellent value. We were both keen to spend a few days in DC as the US Capitol had so much to offer. We had both learnt to embrace and enthuse so much about America, its history, historical characters and constitution over the past six months, but here in the District of Columbia is where the US was born.

Founded by George Washington in 1790 and built on the banks of the Potomac River, the city's grand buildings and monuments were statements not only of America's position in the world order but of power, money and prestige. Stevie and I had agreed a list of places we absolutely had to visit here and hoped three days would be long enough.

We had just about got a grasp of the US legislature of Federal Government, consisting of two chambers, the Lower House of Representatives and the upper chamber called the Senate, all housed in the magnificent architectural masterpiece the Capitol Building on Capitol Hill. Beyond that the workings of the US Government were a complete mystery to me!

On our first day we just decided to familiarise ourselves with the city and its landmarks, bought a dinner of chicken wings and fries in a fast-food joint and slept all night long to catch up on our lost sleep. I didn't realise that a day-and-a-half travelling by Greyhound bus could give you 'jet-lag', but that's what it felt like.

Thursday 24th November was Thanksgiving Day in the USA. From the bunting balloons and excitement in the youth hostel this was shaping to be bigger than Christmas Day. It occurred to us that not much would be open today. Jimmy Carter had decamped to Camp David in Maryland so I guess the White House would be off limits. I had visions of the US President in a two-man tent like me and Stevie but suspected Camp David was in fact somewhat grander. However, after a few enquiries we were assured by a lady at the 'Y' that Camp David was in fact the president's 'country retreat' and grand log cabin built in the 1930s originally for military and secret service agents' use. Our lady friend also assured us the Smithsonian Museum would definitely be open. As the Smithsonian is billed as the world's largest museum we felt it would be a good way to spend the day, especially as it was showery and none too warm outside. Stevie was particularly keen to visit the National Air and Space Museum, where we were told the original Wilbur and Orville Wright plane was exhibited. We were not disappointed, the exhibition was brilliantly arranged. These two guys were the original aeronautical pioneers; the first to invent, build and fly a motor-operated plane – at Kitty Hawk, North Carolina in December 1903; *the Wright Flier*. They also invented aircraft controls that made fixed-wing powered flight possible. The museum had it all. There was so much to see we could have been there all week. After six hours our feet were telling us we had had enough.

Somebody at the hostel had recommended we go down to the Potomac waterfront at Georgetown this evening to 'celebrate' Thanksgiving and said there were was good eating and drinking in the area. They were right. The atmosphere was electric and people were freely wandering around hugging strangers and wishing them 'happy holidays'! Most of the restaurants were way beyond our budget, but we did find a half-decent pizza parlour to eat and hit a few bars. A slightly inebriated guy in his thirties registered our accents and said, 'British right?' Well bugger me with a planting dibber, I thought.

'Yes, correct,' I was delighted someone had got it right at last.

Stevie joined in. 'We've been travelling around North America for over six months and you're the first to call our nationality correctly. Excellent; well done!'

'Oh really?'

'Yep,' said Steve, 'we are normally asked if we are Aussies and on one occasion if we were Swedish.'

'Well I work with a lot of British guys and know the accent. Also been over to London a few times. You guys come from London?'

'No Sussex, south coast opposite France. In fact the French coastline is nearer to us than Trafalgar Square,' I told him.

'Is that right? You guys wanna a beer?'

'We wouldn't say no, thanks,' replied a relieved Steve.

'My name is Carson Capistrano – my friends call me Cap – and this is a pal of mine from the office, Brad Marlborough. We work over in the secretary of state's office over on Pennsylvania Avenue.' We leant over and shook hands. Cap waved a waiter over and ordered four ice-cold Colt Forty-five's and a couple of bags of pretzels.

'So you guys have travelled about a bit,' Stevie started to explain in more detail than I had expected a bit about the last six months, covering twenty-eight US States, five Canadian provinces and as far south as Acapulco in Mexico and many thousands of miles. We had both had a great time and in many ways being asked about it gave opportunity to catalogue some of our adventures in a bit of detail. Steve rambled on about Wawa, Maurice and Yellowstone, the Rockies and Dave Kiln, picking peaches in Osoyoos, Lorraine and Maddison, Becky and Rachael, San Francisco Hippies, Star Trek, Grand Canyon, Monument Valley and down into Mexico and back to New Orleans, not to mention Hannah the Hooker!

'Did you go to Sacramento when you were in California?' asked Brad.

'Not really sure where Sacramento is exactly,' said Steve.

'Oh about eighty miles north-east of Frisco,' came back Brad. 'I'm not surprised you didn't go there; it's not a place tourists would visit. It's the capital of California, one of the least known facts outside of California. In fact many inside have no idea either! No one seems to know it. I worked for the California Legislature before transferring to DC.'

I had a feeling I might regret my next question but couldn't stop myself asking, 'What exactly do you do then?'

Cap snapped back, 'As little as possible! We are pen-pushing, word-processor Federal civil servants and possibly have the most boring jobs in the world and yet we are working in Washington DC for the most powerful nation in the world and being paid big bucks for not very much!' I wasn't sure I wanted to prolong this conversation about US federal civil servants as it seemed rather boring, but asked, 'What do you mean by word processor?'

'Oh it's an aggrandised electric typewriter with a small screen so you can see what you are writing and make corrections, made by IBM.' I was still none the wiser as I didn't understand what he was talking about, but let it go until Stevie chipped in, 'In the UK it's mainly women who type – you know, secretaries and such like.'

I think this slightly offended Brad. 'We do important government work, which I can't go into, but we are a bit more than just secretaries, we have administrative responsibilities.' I could see he was a bit pissed off, so I offered up, 'Well actually my dad can type pretty well. He does notes, minutes and documents for the Parochial Church Council in St Leonards, where we live. He still types with two fingers. He also has one of those duplicating machines to print multiple copies off.'

'So how come your dad is good at typing, if as Stevie here says it's women's work?' asked Cap. He was still clearly needled by Stevie's women's remark.

'Ah well, I can tell you that. He learnt to type during the war as he was in administration.'

'So just like us then,' offered up Cap.

'Well maybe, except he carried his old-fashioned Underwood typewriter from his East London square-bashing barracks to Egypt, on to Sicily, up through Italy, then across to Normandy through France and on to Berlin where he was de-mobbed in 1946.'

'Was he a soldier or a civil servant?' asked Brad.

'Always a soldier first and foremost. He was in the Royal Service Corps, part of the 7th Armoured Division, I used to joke with my mates that Dad fought Hitler off with his typewriter, but I know he had to work very hard in awful makeshift conditions with many 48-hour shifts right through, typing up communiques, dispatches, reports and the like which were sent back to London or HQ, wherever that might have been at any one time.'

This was obviously news to Steve too. He asked me, 'Did he get involved in any actual fighting?'

'I don't actually know. When I was a kid, maybe ten or eleven years old, I rather insensitively asked him if ever killed a German during the war. This visibly annoyed him and he told me to go to bed. I didn't ask again. I had one of those "Action Men" dolls when I was that age. He hated them; brought back bad memories I guess. He was very against me playing with these toys as he said it glorified war. He never wants to talk about anything at all connected to his wartime service. Never has and I guess never will.'

On that sombre note Cap declared it was time for another round of drinks. We said it was our shout.

'Naw; you got to be kidding me,' said Cap.

'What?'

'Let's just say we have got more money than you, after all you two guys haven't got a pot to piss in, you're staying at the 'Y', been sleeping in a tent, hitchhiking everywhere, living on three bucks a day and eating that Dinty Moore crap. If me and Brad can't buy you guys a few beers it would be a Goddam shame. Furthermore, Rich you are the son of a war hero!'

I laughed, 'Put like that, I'll have another Colt 45 please.'

'What about you, Stevie; what did your folks do during the war?' asked Brad.

'Too young. They would have only been about twelve by the time it was all over. My mother was sent out to Herefordshire as a child to live with an old lady called Mrs Gregory. A lot of kids were evacuated from cities to get away from the bombing. She didn't like it much and went back home. Fortunately she never was bombed or I wouldn't be here. Dad lived near Eastbourne so wasn't so much of a problem.'

I decided to turn this round and said to them both. 'Your folks must have been old enough during the war years, what did they do?' This seemed to cause some dilemma and both became evasive and talked round the subject for some time before final commenting that neither was directly involved with the military, citing the family business and careers as taking priority. Lucky bloody them I thought.

Later that evening back at the youth hostel Stevie said, 'I bet those guys were FBI agents. Did you notice the way they played down their role as pen pushers and then said they couldn't talk about their work. They were pretty clean cut and had sharp crewcuts.'

'Look Steve, if those guys were feds, whether off duty or not they wouldn't be allowed to knock back four or five beers like that.'

'I get that, but they did say they worked in Cy Vance's office and not in some anonymous civil service office block somewhere,' insisted Steve.

'Wouldn't the FBI prefer to be anonymous? In any case I don't know and really don't give a flying fuck who they are. What, you think they were lying in wait for us on the off chance we just might stroll into their bar by the Potomac? Come on!'

'Don't be a prick, Wynter,' groaned Steve. 'I didn't suggest they had an official interest in us.'

'Well what is your point then?'

'Just saying, that's all. Strange.'

Stevie and I spent a further three days in DC, really playing the tourists part and made a point of visiting all the key monuments and memorials and re-visited the Smithsonian a couple of times more.

The Washington Monument, the giant Egyptian-style obelisk was mightily impressive – as undoubtedly intended – once the tallest building in the world at five-hundred and fifty-four and-a-half feet, but the Lincoln Memorial was the most poignant with Lincoln sitting upright in his chair inside a Greek-style temple complete with Doric columns, clutching a copy of his famous Gettysburg Address. Between these memorials lies a 2200-foot-long reflection pool, which is brilliant in its conception and does exactly what it was designed to do: reflect the Washington Monument in the sunlight and quite probably the moonlight too. We also went to see the White House but Jimmy was out, so we took a long walk around the perimeter. I had been expecting something to rival Blenheim Palace in Oxfordshire and had to admit to being disappointed. I accept we were standing a long way back, but the White House looked quite insignificant by comparison to Capitol Hill. Maybe Jimmy should insist they swap premises.

14. Founding Fathers and Willie John McBride

On the day we moved on from Washington DC, Monday 27th November, the big news story was the killings of the San Francisco Mayor, George Moscone and his deputy Harvey Milk. Apparently a disgruntled bureaucrat who felt he had been overlooked for promotion took it upon himself to march in to the mayor's office and shoot them both dead at point-blank range – well you could see why he was overlooked! It was of course an appalling and tragic assassination, but all too typical of what we had been reading and hearing about on a fairly constant basis. Colleagues of the dead men conveyed heartfelt tributes and expressed their sorrow and sadness, but to the general populous it was just another couple of insignificant murders and would be very quickly forgotten, as there would always be another shooting round the corner. It just couldn't happen in the UK as no one is allowed to carry guns. Simple solution really.

We were on our final leg to back to New York and ultimately home. We had one further city we wanted to see and that was Philadelphia, one hundred and fifty miles up the road. There were half-empty Greyhound buses running every half hour up to Philly, so we just jumped on one at our convenience, mid-morning. To get full value from our bus passes we would only be able to spend 36 hours in Philadelphia and what a great day and a half we had.

The city of the founding fathers exceeded all expectations. Inevitably it was incredibly modern and crammed with skyscrapers, but it also retained and valued its heritage and original buildings such as the Declaration House where Thomas Jefferson wrote the Declaration of Independence, Independence Hall with its mighty clock tower, the House of the American Revolution, Benjamin Franklin's home and the magnificent Christ Church. All these ancient buildings surrounded by modern-day booming tower blocks, a contrast to behold. When I say ancient, one does have to keep perspective; most of them were maybe a hundred to a hundred and thirty years old. But it was the sense of scale which fascinated me, as the old buildings were so small and mainly red brick compared with the massive window-clad office blocks which cocooned them. The proportions were all wrong.

It was amazing really, after six months of discovering so many new and varied experiences, landscapes and architecture, I could still be overawed on nearly a daily basis, which just demonstrated the vastness and variety of the American continent.

Stevie had called home from Washington and said we would likely be back next week and we were rapidly running out of money. To Stevie's surprise his dad wired him some money, about a hundred quid, which we had to cash at the First National bank. This took most of the afternoon. While the cash was very welcome and much needed, it was frustrating to waste time hanging about a bank. It was also an unwanted debt I would have to settle sooner rather than later. It would be an awkward conversation with my own dad when I got back home, asking him to advance £50 to pay back Stevie's father.

We were lucky to find an affordable downtown hotel for one night and rebalanced our budget by eating at Burger King. The next morning we wasted no time on the tourist trail. The Liberty Bell was our first port of call; famed for its crack, it is a symbol of American independence and democracy and best of all was free to view. In fact most of Philly was free to view, including some museums. There were exhibitions of the American Revolution and the Civil War. I hadn't appreciated the city's role in the development of the United States; so many of the early presidents came from Philadelphia and the surrounding area. Most famously of all was the signing here of the Declaration of Independence in 1776.

Founded by a Quaker, William Penn, in the mid-eighteenth century on the Delaware River, it developed into one of the most important trading ports and became one of the first industrialised American cities. Philadelphia was a hub for immigrants in the nineteenth century, especially Irish, Italian and German and later Africans. On the outskirts of the city there are still many old Victorian-style mansions which reflect the wealth and vast fortunes the many successful merchants made. I found a lot of them somewhat austere and a bit spooky. One or two looked more like cricket pavilions you might find at the more prestigious clubs back home such as Aigburth home of Liverpool Cricket Club. But they had survived development and were still here, which was great. I only hope they have some sort of preservation order on them.

I really liked Philly, it was impressive but the Big Apple beckoned so we decided to max out our Greyhound pass and took a bus at a very unsociable hour which brought us into Manhattan at eight in the morning. Close to the bus station was an awful looking downmarket hotel, which we thought would suit our budget perfectly. It did. It was dirt cheap because the dirt was spread throughout the hotel evenly. The Kempster Hotel had a damp musty smell with a few years' layers of cobwebs and grime. The guy behind reception desk, which was nothing more than an unvarnished plank of wood, was equally damp and musty. I suspected he had cobwebs under his armpits and shit for brains. He answered to the name Harry and told us it would cost $7 a night each if we shared a room and breakfast was extra. There was no chance of us buying breakfast here; we wanted to live! The threadbare carpets were so damp you could grow cress on them. In fact there was enough dirt and moisture in the room to establish a small allotment. We knew we weren't going to enjoy this hotel; it was just a hotel of convenience and cheap rates and free rats, so as a bit of fun we registered under the names of Tom Spencer and Willie John McBride. Spencer was a mundane, but well-respected professional cricket umpire back home who out in the middle came across as cheerless and without character. Although it was possibly an illusion, he didn't appear to have any teeth and chewed continuously so consequently his face creased up and he looked more like Albert Steptoe in a white cap. Willie John on the other hand, Stevie's alias, was a gargantuan Irishman from Belfast who captained the British Lions successfully on tours to South Africa and New Zealand and was rightly held in high esteem by the world of rugby. Stevie just loved the name Willie John McBride, and Tom Spencer was probably my polar opposite in terms of personality and rather cynically I regarded him as a figure of fun, although I knew him to be a top-class umpire. So as Spencer and McBride we signed in the Kempster Hotel for three nights. A *'Hotel of Distinction'* it read outside. It certainly was that, but perhaps not as originally intended.

We went straight to visit 42nd Street and 5th Avenue as the grandee address of Manhattan. I immersed myself in record shops and decided buy a couple of albums to take home on Sunday as they were such good prices. There were albums I had heard over the past few months and had grown to appreciate and would undoubtedly hold great memories for me in the future.

Court and Spark by Joni Mitchell, Wish You Were Here by Pink Floyd, plus the new Grateful Dead album Shakedown Street, released last week. I knew they would always remind of the many great places and good times we had enjoyed during our time in Canada and Stateside. Sadly and as much as I admired Gary Brown, I couldn't bring myself to buy a copy of *La Vaselina*; what on earth would JJ Eaton-Rye say!

We were feeling a bit tired after a long night on the bus so decided to go to the cinema just off

Broadway, partly to rest up and get out of the rain, but partly to see the much-heralded Clint Eastwood film *Every Which Way but Loose*. To our amazement the big bare-knuckle fight scene was staged in the centre of Jacksons Hole, Wyoming. We recognised so much of the town and the places we had seen there, not least the cattle-horn arch in the main square. Bloody good movie too! We had to have an early night but I didn't trust the bed sheets. I thought there was a fairly good chance of bed bugs, so used my sleeping bag. It was just as well, as it was not exactly warm in New York on the last day of November.

The following day we fell in with the tourists and went to the Empire State Building, which when first built was the world's tallest building. Remarkably this classic Art Deco building was constructed and opened in under fourteen months. Over a hundred floors tall with a fabulous observation deck including an external balcony on the 86th floor, the views from the top were quite astonishing. We were fortunate it was quite a clear day if somewhat cold. We could see the island of Manhattan mapped out in front and indeed behind us like a scale model. The twin towers of the World Trade Centre loomed in front of us in Lower Manhattan. We could look across to Brooklyn in the east and to Jersey in the west. On top is a huge antenna for broadcasting. The world's first FM radio was broadcast from the Empire State in 1940. We had great views of the equally Art Deco Chrysler Building with its ornate roof. From ground level it looks like a space rocket.

Later we took the subway to take a stroll in Central Park but we were distracted by a futuristic modern cylindrical building, the Guggenheim museum. We were told it housed contemporary art; that certainly wasn't our sort of thing so didn't bother to go in but the outside was fascinating. It was an architectural conundrum as the swirling round shape was wider at the top than it was at the base. Designed by Frank Lloyd Wright, it is over twenty-five years old but looked as though it was constructed yesterday. Not so far away was the great Carnegie Hall where the legendary Ray Charles was billed to play this very evening. The gig was sold out, which was just as well given the price of the tickets, but it would have been great to have gone to a concert in this iconic venue and seen Ray Charles perform.

Today, Sunday 3rd December, was going to be our last full day. Stevie and I agreed we had to visit the Statue of Liberty as probably the most famous of all American symbols. For the many millions of newcomers arriving in the USA from the late nineteenth century onwards, the Statue of Liberty was the first thing they would have seen when arriving in New York as the vast majority of immigrants did.

We took a ferry from Battery Park to the Statue of Liberty on Liberty Island. On arrival we paid a couple of bucks entry and we were ushered into the museum in the base of the statue, which struck me as quite enormous. It exhibited many clear black-and-white pictures of the original immigration processing building for all the new arrivals on Ellis Island next door and of the many boats and liners which sailed in from Europe and the UK carrying thousands of hopeful people embarking on a new life the other side of the Atlantic Ocean, including my own grandmother and her many siblings. There was also a great sequence of pictures of the construction of the Statue of Liberty. It was actually made in France and shipped over in vast crates. All the Yanks had to do was manufacture a giant concrete plinth on which to construct it.

Formally opened on 28th October 1886, it was presented as a gift from France, as a gift of friendship and built by Gustave Eiffel, he of Eiffel Tower fame. Made of copper, it stands 305 feet tall including the pedestal; the statue is of a robed Roman goddess with her right arm held aloft holding a torch. In her left hand she clutches a tableau of the US Declaration of Independence. She represents an 'icon of freedom' to welcome the immigrants to American shores. We then climbed the metal internal stairways right to the top where we could take in the great views out to sea from inside the statue's tiara. It did actually seem strange that after virtually 200 days in Canada, the US and Mexico to approach the Statue of Liberty last and from the rear, so to speak. What I can you tell though, it was bloody freezing up there!

Back on Manhattan we headed back towards Fifth Avenue and took a good look up and down Broadway. It certainly did have a lot of glamour about it but – and I maybe biased – I didn't think it had quite the cachet of the London's West End or Covent Garden. Maybe it was the weather or the realisation that tomorrow I would be home, but it all felt a little flat. However, we agreed we had to go out with a bang, so decided to head for Greenwich Village. We were looking for a joint called Café Wha, where back in the sixties Dylan, Hendrix and Lou Reed and the Velvet Underground all played. We were told it was on MacDougal Street, but had closed some years back and turned into a restaurant specialising in Arab food and music. I couldn't think of anything worse. However, the area was jammed with bars, eateries and live-music clubs, not to mention numerous discos. We found an interesting-looking bar playing a good combination of rock and blues. The fast food suited our budget and beer was inexpensive. The place was busy and we got the impression everybody knew everybody else in there. In fact while the vast majority were American and a high percentage of them were New Yorkers, they were in reality all strangers mingling and talking with each other. Very soon we started to integrate and fought off girls wanting to know if we were Australians. We had built immunity to this question and just avoided giving a direct answer. We really couldn't care less where people thought we were from anymore. The food was good enough and the beers flowed, the music played and we exchanged stories, banter and jokes with a wide range of people all out for a good time. Stevie was very keen to pull a bird on our last night, with my full support I might add, but unfortunately it didn't happen. Maybe it was just as well, as trying to impress a girl at the awful Kempster Hotel would have been a challenge in itself. Approaching midnight, feeling slightly the worse for wear, we staggered back to the dreaded Kempster dumpster only to find the front door locked and bolted. We banged on the door hard and yelled up at the first floor. After five minutes the Hackneyed 'shit for brains' Harry, the foul-smelling receptionist opened a third floor window.

'What the fuck doya you guys want?' he bellowed.

'We wanna come in,' shouted back Steve. 'We're staying here.'

'Oh yeah? Got any ID?'

'No,' I shouted back. 'We're Tom Spencer and Willie John McBride. Our ID is in our room,' I lied.

Steve started giggling which really didn't help.

'Look don't you recognise us, we checked in a couple of days ago with you. You know, the Australians.'

This finished Steve off, he was laughing out loud now and I started to come out in sympathy and spluttered and choked as I tried to hold back my laughter.

'Look for Christsakes man, you can't leave us on the fucking pavement all night. We paid you $14 for the fucking shithole of a room. Now open up.'

My threatening abuse seemed to qualify me as a Kempster resident and a couple of minutes later Harry reluctantly opened the door and we barged past. As we didn't have ID to show him, we barricaded ourselves in our disgusting room.

The following morning, having overslept, we took the subway up to Queens where we had to find the Laker SkyTrain Office. Fortunately we found it without too much difficulty and secured two tickets for the evening's return flight to Gatwick. With at least seven-and-a-half hours to kill we went back to Times Square for brunch and coffee and almost on a whim decided to march across the Brooklyn Bridge just for the hell of it.

The Brooklyn Bridge, with its Gothic-shaped arches and suspension cables, is one of New York's most recognised landmarks, spanning the East River from Manhattan to Brooklyn. Completed in 1883, it was the world's first steel suspension bridge. The central span is 1,595 ft long by 85 ft wide. It can be seen from many of the ferries and the east side of Manhattan. In terms of wow factor it sure did knock 'London Bridge' into a cocked hat.

It took us well over an hour to complete the walk both ways but was well worth it, despite the biting cold and a fierce wind. We were on a wooden walkway, which ran above the six lanes of non-stop traffic below. At the main pillars at the central point there is a viewing platform, where we could see the granite towers up close.

From the bridge are beautiful views over Manhattan, the East River, and beyond to the Statue of Liberty. We waved farewell to the Roman goddess and at one point I thought she waved back to us. Maybe she was thanking us for visiting America.

Late afternoon we returned to the SkyTrain office at Queens and took a courtesy bus out to JFK Airport with an assortment of Brits, Europeans and American passengers. After a rather boring three hours drinking Johnny Walker Red Label from our duty-free bottle, inside the departure hall we boarded our 10.30 flight. It was a strange sensation sitting on plane thinking what lay ahead of me back home. It was a long and boring flight and in my mind I was wondering if I could stay at home after all I had experienced over the last six or seven months. Should I at least have a place of my own now? It had many advantages in terms of personal freedom and not having my father hassling me all the time. The downside of course it would cost a lot more than living at home but I knew I would have to take flight sometime, so it may as well be sooner rather than later. Of course I wanted to see my parents and friends again, I was looking forward to it, there was so much to tell them. But the thought of a job with South-East Gas sent a cold shiver down my spine. Clearly I did have to get a job, which wouldn't necessarily be easy. I had successfully put my career dilemma on the back burner the last six months, but now reality was catching up with me again. Maybe I was coming to a crossroads and returning to Hastings to face my demons. In terms of academic qualifications, not much had changed, I had to play to my strengths. I suppose I was heading home with considerably more life experience and a new-found love of travelling, which I had found both liberating and exhilarating and knew that life on the road had really suited me. I also knew I could sell, as Mum had told me many times I would have sold my own grandmother given half a chance and old Aunty Val said I had the gift of the gab – whatever that meant – so I guess that will be the direction I would have to look at. A career in sales, travelling all over the country actually seemed quite appealing depending on what I was selling, especially if I could secure a fully-expensed company car.

As we came in to land, the gloom over Gatwick fitted my mood but I knew it was time to shake myself down and out of the doldrums. The lad from Hastings had grown up and was now a man with a plan.

Once through the UK passport control we caught a train from Gatwick back down to Bexhill and Hastings. Waiting on a freezing cold Gatwick platform we decided to break the train journey at Haywards Heath and call into the nearest pub for good old pint of much missed English bitter for a celebration drink. We hoisted our backpacks across our shoulders and strode out of Haywards Heath station straight in to the pub opposite, the Burrell Arms.

There weren't many people in the bar at 11.30 in the morning but there was one old colonel sporting a cravat and a silver Rolex, propping up the bar, with his early morning snifter, chatting up the barmaid. We leant our backpacks against the bar and raised our pints in a sort of victory salute to the last seven months.

'Typical bloody Australians,' commented the sniffy colonel to no one in particular.

THE END

Accreditations

I have two people to thank specifically for their support and stimulation during the writing of this book. Firstly Francesca Green whose sometimes fierce critical eye pointed out glaring errors and offered constructive direction. My wife Jackie for unequivocal support and encouragement and her excellent front cover design.

I would also like to thank Felicity Fair Thompson and Hugh Griffiths whose advice and encouragement I found invaluable. David Walshaw at New Generation Publishing for guiding me through the murky waters of book publication and marketing. Also Linda Harris whose proof reading has proved invaluable.

I have changed the names of most of the characters in this book to protect their anonymity and dignity. Any resemblance to any living or deceased person is therefore totally coincidental and unintended. Any factual or grammatical mistakes I take full responsibility for.

95% of the *Hitch America* story is true. Looking back at it now forty-three years on, I can't believe I actually did it. But I did.

Printed in Great Britain
by Amazon